HELPFUL REFLECTIONS
for Difficult Times

HELPFUL REFLECTIONS
for Difficult Times

Ed Keelen

A combination of the author's own original reflections about how a Christian copes with difficult times, augmented by his favorite Christian authors through direct quotations and paraphrasing of their key concepts

AMBASSADOR INTERNATIONAL
GREENVILLE, SOUTH CAROLINA & BELFAST, NORTHERN IRELAND

www.ambassador-international.com

Helpful Reflections for Difficult Times

Unless otherwise indicated, Scripture is taken from the New Revised Standard Version Bible, copyright ©1989 the Division of Christian Education of the National Council of the Churches of Christ in the United States of America. Used by permission. All rights reserved.

Scripture marked KJV taken from The King James Version, The Authorized Version. Public Domain.

ISBN: 978-1-62020-843-4

eISBN: 978-1-62020-854-0

Cover Design and Page Layout by Hannah Nichols

eBook Conversion by Anna Riebe Raats

AMBASSADOR INTERNATIONAL
Emerald House
411 University Ridge, Suite B14
Greenville, SC 29601, USA
www.ambassador-international.com

AMBASSADOR BOOKS
The Mount
2 Woodstock Link
Belfast, BT6 8DD, Northern Ireland, UK
www.ambassadormedia.co.uk

The colophon is a trademark of Ambassador, a Christian publishing company.

DEDICATION

This book is dedicated to my wife Cathy, who has been there for me during my own difficult times.

FOREWORD

MANY YEARS AGO, MY WIFE and I and some friends toured a winery in Napa Valley, California. Near the end of our tour, we were taken to an observation deck overlooking most of the vineyard. Referring to a map of the property, our guide pointed out the locations of the varieties of grapes, and we were told that, although the rich soil and climate of the valley were ideal for growing grapes, the best wine came from the mountainside. There, the soil was rocky and thinner; the temperatures varied, and the vines were under greater stress. One of our friends immediately commented that this reminded her of her faith. The difficulty and distress of everyday life can, like the vines growing on the mountainside, deepen and strengthen our belief in God.

Ed Keelen has been a close and treasured friend and mentor for more than twenty-five years, and his life experiences have made his faith one of the best "wines" I know. After being diagnosed and treated with two forms of cancer within two years and suffering permanent and serious damage to his kidneys, Ed used his recovery to deepen his relationship with God. Although I think he would admit to a season of questioning "why me?," rather than rebel, Ed channeled his energy into the several years process of writing *Helpful Reflections for Difficult Times*.

After going through cancer and other complications myself in 2007, I was privileged to be in a study group with Ed and two other close friends for approximately ten years. During those regular and very meaningful times, I personally experienced and benefited from Ed's wisdom and counsel. I believe the reflections he has now put to words were built upon the thoughts and prayers that were so helpful to me during my own times of doubt and despair.

Whether you are going through a time of disease, suffering, loneliness, or the loss of a loved one, Ed's reflections, meditations and prayers that follow will surely be a source of comfort and hope: comfort in the knowledge that the God of all comfort is with you throughout the entire process and in the hope that this time will soon be over.

—TOM FALLS

May 7, 2018

I. GETTING STARTED

Romans 8:28. *We know that all things work together for good for those who love God, who are called according to his purpose.*

You are going through a difficult time and have turned to this book for guidance. It is an excellent start to your recovery. Hopefully, you have carved out a specific time and place each day to read these reflections and are coupling it with a time of prayer and silence before God. It will become one of the most important times in your day. You are practicing the spiritual discipline of meditation, which will help you cope with the day-to-day pressures and difficulties that you are experiencing. Read today's verse aloud and pause to reflect on it. God is good; God works for your good. Despite how distant and uncaring He may seem at this point in your life, know that He loves you and can do only good. You may even be angry with God for the circumstances He has put you in. That's OK; express your anger to Him in your prayers: He knows how you feel and cares about you. As we progress through this book, you will begin to understand the breadth and depth of God's love, how much He cares for you, and how He carries you through difficult circumstances.

PRAYER: Thank You, Lord, for this time of devotion and meditation. May it help to heal my wounds and help me to love and serve You all the more. In Jesus' name, amen.

2. REJOICE IN OUR SUFFERING

Romans 5:3b-4. *We also boast in our sufferings, knowing that suffering produces endurance, and endurance produces character, and character produces hope.*

Perhaps your difficult time involves some sort of suffering. It is easy to recognize our sufferings, but to rejoice in them as this verse commands is quite another matter! It requires an attempt to look at things from God's perspective: life is short in comparison to the eternity that we will spend with God. And, just as Christ suffered, so we must suffer. But the ultimate outcome of suffering is for our good—we will learn how to persevere. We are in this life for the long haul, and God gives us the patience to endure. We will build character—become more Christ-like, more humble, with a servant's attitude. We will have hope—things will get better, if not in this lifetime, then in the life to come. And, we have fellow Christians here and now who can help us endure whatever suffering befalls us.

PRAYER: Lord, sometimes when I am suffering, it is difficult to see Your hand at work. Bring the comfort of other Christians to my side and give me Your perspective so that I can rejoice in Your goodness and grace. In Jesus' name, amen.

3. MANAGING ANGER

James 1:19-20. *You must understand this, my beloved: let everyone be quick to listen, slow to speak, slow to anger; for your anger does not produce God's righteousness.*

In your difficult time, it is so easy to get angry about a situation: "road rage," an injustice done to you, something that someone says that rubs you the wrong way. One time, a coworker said something that embarrassed me in front of my colleagues. It really got to me in an unhealthy way, as the anger boiled up inside me. But anger is not God's way. Instead, be "quick to listen, slow to speak, and slow to anger." Hard to do? Yes. But start by counting to ten when you feel anger welling up inside you and seek out someone's counsel whom you trust. After the meeting, I consulted with a business associate about the incident, and he assured me that I had taken my colleagues comment out of context and no harm was meant by it. By concentrating on listening to your trusted friend, your anger will dissipate. Sure, occasionally, you're going to "blow your stack." You're only human. But, as you reflect on this verse, your tendency toward anger will lessen, and you will begin to "bring about the righteous life that God desires."

PRAYER: Lord, Help me to count to ten when I am starting to get angry, and to seek out a friend that I can listen to for advice. I want to curb my anger and serve You. In Jesus' name, amen.

4. GOD'S WISDOM

Daniel 2:21. *[God] changes times and seasons, deposes kings and sets up kings; he gives wisdom to the wise and knowledge to those who have understanding.*

David DeWitt says that wisdom comes when we understand the patterns of God.[1] God "changes times and seasons." God Himself is unchanging, but He loves to see change in us, and we become wise when we understand these patterns of change and incorporate them into our daily lives. What are some of these patterns of change? The seasons of the year themselves, the joyful times and the sad times, the lonely times and the social times; times of stress and times of relaxation; times of grieving and of celebrating. Read Ecclesiastes 3:1-8 for a wonderful description of God's patterns and the changes He invokes in our lives ("To everything, there is a season"). Wisdom is knowing what phase of the cycle you are in. If it is a positive part of the cycle, relish it, but do not take it for granted or take credit for it. If it is a negative part of the cycle such as you are experiencing in your difficult time, have hope that "this too, shall pass" and a positive time will come. I am a cancer survivor and, of course, found myself in the negative part of the cycle. But, by relying on my friends and my church life, I was able to see things in perspective and look beyond the suffering phase with the hope that I would get better and once again enjoy life to the fullest. Now, post-cancer, I can look back on that experience as a time of intense spiritual growth and see God's hand pulling me through it into the positive part of the cycle.

PRAYER: Lord, I thank You for the seasons in my life. Help me to embrace change and to recognize Your hand in all things. Knowing Your patterns is the beginning of wisdom. In Jesus' name, amen.

---

1   David DeWitt, "The Mature Man," *Promises to Keep*, 46.

5. THE PEACEABLE FRUIT OF RIGHTEOUSNESS

Hebrews 12:11 (KJV). *Now no chastening for the present seemeth to be joyous, but grievous: nevertheless, afterward it yieldeth the peaceable fruit of righteousness unto them which are exercised thereby.*

When I was going through my cancer treatments, I carried this verse in my wallet and referred to it frequently. When you are suffering, it is a grievous matter—you want it to end. But with this verse in mind, you can make it through your suffering because you can look forward to the "peaceable fruit of righteousness" once you have gone through your trial. This is a Biblical promise. We will experience the "peaceable fruit of righteousness" at the end of our suffering, whether in this life or our eternal life with God: only God knows. But it is a verse to sustain us. There is a light at the end of the tunnel, and it is Christ's light, not the light of an oncoming train!

PRAYER: Lord, it is hard to go through this time of testing, but I embrace Your promise that when it is over, I will experience the "peaceable fruit of righteousness." Thank You for that promise. In Jesus' name, amen.

6. COMMUNING WITH NATURE

Job 12:7-9. But ask the animals, and they will teach you; the birds of the air, and they will tell you; ask the plants of the earth, and they will teach you, and the fish of the sea will declare to you. Who among all these does not know that the hand of the Lord has done this?

Communing with nature is one of the best ways to cope with your difficult time and draw close to God. The beauty that surrounds us could not have been created randomly or by accident. At dawn or sunset, God colors the sky with a marvelous and varied tapestry of clouds and the unique way the sun's rays cascade off them. In the woods, we are surrounded by a cacophony of sounds, including our own walk as we rustle through the leaves or hear the sound of breaking twigs under our feet. There are endless species of birds, animals and insects to amuse or fascinate us. "Who among all these does not know that the hand of the Lord has done this?" Despite whatever troubles you face, spend time outside, communing with God. Compared to the grandeur of God's creation, your troubles won't seem quite so insurmountable.

PRAYER: Lord, Thank You for the splendor of nature and how readily available it is for me to enjoy. Yours is a magnificent creation, and, in comparison, it makes my troubles seem less formidable. In Jesus' name, amen.

7. THE TRUE NATURE OF GOD

Matthew 11:29. *Take my yoke upon you, and learn from me; for I am gentle and humble in heart, and you will find rest for your souls.*

This verse reminds us of the true nature of God: He is "gentle and humble in heart." It is perhaps difficult to see God in this light: so often in the Old Testament He is depicted as a harsh, judgmental God. That is one of the main reasons God sent Jesus to be with us; to show us His true nature. Perhaps the following story, whose origin I don't know, provides a good analogy. In a recent war, a group of soldiers got detached from their unit and were taken prisoner by the enemy. They were kept in cramped quarters, fed meager portions, and they eventually lost hope that they would be rescued. Finally, a group of storm troopers got word of their whereabouts and overcame their captors and stormed into the room where the soldiers were huddled together. The soldiers were frightened by the storm troopers, who wore gas masks and a full armament of protective gear. They cowered in the corner and refused to be rescued. Finally, one of the storm troopers removed his gas mask and protective gear and knelt down beside them and started talking calmly to them. Through his actions, the soldiers became convinced that the storm troopers were there to rescue them, and they followed them out of the room to safety. God is like the storm troopers: hard to understand, sometimes appearing cold and judgmental. Jesus is like the trooper who knelt beside the captives to show them His true nature so that they might believe and be rescued.

PRAYER: Lord, Thank You for coming to earth and showing us God's true nature. Help me to reflect on God's goodness during difficult times. Through Your kindness, love, and grace we are rescued! In Jesus' name, amen.

8. WHAT HAS PERMANENCE?

Psalm 20:7. *Some take pride in chariots, and some in horses, but our pride is in the name of the Lord our God.*

We all like our shiny new cars and new houses and other material things. But these things have no permanence in our lives. One hundred years from now, that car will likely be a piece of rusted junk in a scrap yard, and the house may very well have been torn down to make way for something more modern. What does have permanence? The name of the Lord our God. He is the Alpha and Omega, the Beginning and the End, and we can put our trust in Him. There is a whole spiritual world out there of which we get only glimpses, and yet, ultimately, it will be more real to us than what we possess now. Pray. Meditate. Let go of "things." Cherish your relationship with the Lord our God, especially in times of difficulty. When I got my first computer, I was "hooked" and spent hours playing with it. It began to take away from my prayer and meditation time and supplant my spiritual life. I finally realized what was happening, broke myself of the computer habit, and re-dedicated myself to my prayer and meditation time. I let go of something temporal for a spirituality that adds meaning to my life and gives me assurance in God's provision for my life both now and in the future.

PRAYER: Lord, Help me to see You in a new light, in a place of permanence in my life. I must let go of my obsession with material things and turn to You as my source of strength. In Jesus' name, amen.

9. OBEYING THE LORD'S COMMANDS

John 14:21. They *who have my commandments and keep them are those who love me; and those who love me will be loved by my Father, and I will love them and reveal myself to them.*

The pathway to love (and a way to overcome your difficult time) is through knowing God's commands and obeying them. How do we know God's commands? By reading His Word—the Bible. Not only just by reading, but also by taking the words to heart with the help of the Holy Spirit. This means memorizing verses that are meaningful to us so that they can be brought to immediate recall when we are in distress or need God's solace. Once we "have" the Lords commands, we obey them. Not because we must, but out of love for our Savior and our desire to serve Him. Yes, we will fall short of obeying every command—we are human and sinful, but that's OK—God's grace and the sacrifice of His Son on our behalf are sufficient. He loves us unconditionally, just as we are. When we fall short, we confess our sins and are assured of God's forgiveness (Rom. 10:9). Then we repent and make every effort not to make the same mistake.

PRAYER: Lord, Thank You for loving us and showing Yourself to us when we take in Your Word and obey Your commands. Thank You also that You have made provision when we fall short and for Your unconditional love. In Jesus' name, amen.

10. THE "I AND THOU" RELATIONSHIP

Matthew 6:9b-13 (KJV). Our Father which art in heaven, Hallowed be thy name. Thy kingdom come, Thy will be done in earth, as it is in heaven. Give us this day our daily bread. And forgive us our debts, as we forgive our debtors. And lead us not into temptation, but deliver us from evil: for thine is the kingdom, and the power, and the glory forever. Amen.

The essence of our glorifying God is in our personal relationship to Him. Martin Buber talks about three types of relationships: "I-It" relationships, "I-You" relationships, and "Us-Them" relationships.[2] The "I-It" relationship treats other persons as objects to be used to further your own interests. "What can you do for me?" is the operative question. The "I-You" relationship recognizes the mutual reward and growth that comes from valuing the other person and the relationship. "How can we help each other" is the operative question. The "Us-Them" relationship thinks that I am right, and you are wrong—it pits us against each other to see who is superior. Wars are a good example of an "Us-Them" relationships. It asks, "How can I exert my power over you?" It goes without saying that the ideal Christian relationship, and the one you want to cultivate in your difficult time, is the "I-You" relationship of mutual respect and growth. Since our relationship to God is a personal one, it should be an "I-You" relationship too; or, because God is so Holy we might call it an *I and Thou* relationship, which is the title of Buber's book.

PRAYER: Dear Lord, I very much desire an *I and Thou* relationship with You. I know that You care about me personally, and I cherish my prayer time with You, communing with You through nature, and the myriad of ways You reveal Yourself to me. In Jesus' name, amen.

---

2   Martin Buber, *I and Thou* (New York, Charles Scribner's Sons, 1958); This book deals with the concepts listed.

II. FELLOWSHIP IN CHURCH

Acts 9:31. *Meanwhile the church throughout Judea, Galilee, and Samaria had peace and was built up. Living in the fear of the Lord and in the comfort of the Holy Spirit, it increased in numbers.*

If you are going through a difficult time, being a member of a church is a tremendous help. In fact, if you aren't a member of a church, you aren't practicing the fullness of Christianity. Granted, there is an important element of your faith that is yours alone: to walk in communion and fellowship with your Lord Jesus Christ and to know Him personally. But that is only part of the story. The other part is the communion and fellowship that you share with other Christians who are in the faith journey with you. They will pray for you in times of need, break bread with you in time of fellowship, worship God with you at the appointed time on Sunday, and learn more about Jesus with you in Sunday School. They will be Christ to you. But beyond the visible fellowship that is provided by the church, there is an invisible element to church that is equally, if not more, important. Eugene Peterson in his book, *Practice Resurrection* says this:

> Church is also something we can't see. We can't see the ascension of Jesus. We can't see "the descent of the dove." We can't see sins washed away. We can't see the birth of a soul. We can't see the river of life. It is not uncommon for people to walk into a church out of curiosity, look around, leave, and later report to their friends, "I couldn't see that there is anything to it." That is also a very unspiritual thing to say, for a great deal of what we live by is unseen, the air we breathe and the promises we make, for a start.[3]

Cherish the visible and invisible elements of church. It is a wonderful gift to us. It is the Body of Christ.

PRAYER: Dear Lord, Sometimes it is hard for me to go to church. Help me to recognize both the visible and invisible elements of church and to embrace its mystery as well as the wonderful communion of saints that it provides. In Jesus' name, amen.

---

3   Eugene H. Peterson, *Practice Resurrection: A Conversation on Growing Up in Christ* (Grand Rapids, Wm. B. Eerdmans, 2010), Kindle, 1422.

12. PEACE IN THE THICK OF BATTLE

Romans 1:7b. *Grace to you and peace from God our Father and the Lord Jesus Christ.*

Sometimes we think that the peace of God is being serene ourselves: calm, collected, totally relaxed, zzzz . . . But Frederick Buechner provides a new aspect of being at peace with God—being fully engaged![4] Think of being in the thick of the battle. Recall athletes who are "in the zone." Recall a time when you never felt more alive than when the adrenaline was pumping, and you were making rapid fire decisions that felt "right" in your gut, and everybody was in sync and paying attention to you and doing just the right thing. That is the peace of God, too! I had never thought of it that way—that peace can come from being highly energized and full of life and in the thick of things. But, God wants us to use our creativity and God-given talents, and I think He is very pleased when we are being fully deployed in this way. During difficult times, it is sometimes hard to be "up" for things, but you should make every effort to be energized and experience this new aspect of being at peace with God. The fullest expression of this peace is when we deploy it for the benefit of others. Buechner says, "to journey for the sake of saving our lives is little by little to cease to live in any sense that matters, even to ourselves. It is only by journeying for the world's sake (for others) that little by little we start to come alive." So, the peace of God which passes all understanding is being in the thick of battle—being so fully enmeshed in a circumstance that you forget yourself and become fully devoted to the cause at hand. And it has its fullest expression when our devotion is not just for ourselves, but for the world's sake.

PRAYER: Dear Lord, Thank You for all the gifts and talents You have given me. Help me to use them to the fullest, so that I may experience this aspect of the peace of God. In Jesus' name, amen.

---

4 Frederick Buechner, *Listening to Your Life: Daily Meditations with Frederick Buechner* (New York: HarperCollins, 1992), 22.

13. THE ORGANIC GARDEN

Jeremiah 29:11. *For surely I know the plans I have for you, says the Lord, plans for your welfare and not for harm, to give you a future with hope.*

Of all the metaphors for life with Christ, I think I like the organic garden metaphor the best. There is much beauty in an organic garden, but, while some plants are thriving and revealing their beauty, others are struggling, decaying and dying. They are every bit as necessary to the vitality of the garden as the plants that are thriving, for in death, they provide the food and nourishment upon which the thriving plants depend. The life/death process of the organic garden must be seen in its entirety before the whole garden can be truly appreciated. So it is in life. We go through the cycles of good times, sometimes called "resurrection times," and difficult times, "crucifixion times." God sees the whole picture and declares it "good." When we are going through the difficult times, it is often hard to see the goodness in God's creation. But it is there. There is always something to be thankful for, and often it is for other people whose turn it is to thrive in the organic garden of life. God sees the whole picture, and He has a plan for our lives. Trust in His ultimate wisdom to see you through your difficult time.

PRAYER: Dear Lord, Thank You for being able to see the whole picture and how I fit in it. From my limited perspective, I don't understand the trials You put me through, but You have a plan for my life, and it is good. In Jesus' name, amen.

14. LIVING DAY TO DAY

Matthew 6:34. *So do not worry about tomorrow, for tomorrow will bring worries of its own. Today's trouble is enough for today.*

Are you so focused on achieving a goal or getting over your difficult time that you lose sight of the enjoyment of living day to day? Patrick Morley says, "it is engaging and enjoying the process of living out our lives day by day—enjoying each step along the way—that makes us happy."[5] According to Morley, we can't control the future. We can't possibly know what God has in store for us. Sometimes, people think that if only they had "the right information," they could control the future outcome of events. With a process-oriented focus rather than a results-oriented focus, we can let go of the false sense of self control that we think we have over our lives, and let God guide the process. That is not to say that you shouldn't have goals in life. It is always good to have something to plan for and hope for and feel good about when you achieve it. But don't let goals govern your life to the point where they preclude other opportunities that God has in mind. Stay flexible. Live in the moment, alive to the process that God is laying out before you. Morley concludes, "we often spend much of our time stewing over that which we will never know until it happens. Would it not be more useful to once and for all accept the fact that the future is the secret of God, and then live by faith, trusting that because God is good, our future will end 'good'? What a comfort to trust and rest in the sovereignty of a good God."[6]

PRAYER: Dear Lord, Help me to live in the moment and enjoy the process of living, and not worry so much about the future. The future is in Your hands, and You promise that it will be "good." In Jesus' name, amen.

---

5   Patrick Morley, *Ten Secrets for the Man in the Mirror* (Grand Rapids: Zondervan, 2000), 47.
6   Morley, 47.

15. EXPERIENCING JOY

1 Thessalonians 3:9. *How can we thank God enough for you in return for all the joy we feel before our God because of you?*

Eugene Peterson points out that in going through your difficult time, you may have fleeting times of happiness—a good meal that your wife has cooked, a good report card from your children, a memorable, calming walk through the woods. However, you can have constant times of joy—even in times of suffering. Happiness is more driven by external things and our response to them; joy is experienced internally and comes from God. Can we will ourselves to be joyful? Certainly not. It is the product of abundant Christian living. It can be urged to come to us when we fill our minds with the stories of God's acts and have a thankful attitude for the blessings we do have. I think that joy and thankfulness go hand in hand. But, as Peterson points out, "Joy is not a requirement of Christian discipleship; it is a consequence. It is not what we have to acquire in order to experience life in Christ; it is what comes to us when we are walking in the way of faith and obedience . . . Joy is a product of abundance; it is the overflow of vitality."[7] We can't be joyful all the time any more than we can be happy all the time. But we *can* be joyful at times when we are not able to be happy. How is this possible? Peterson describes it as "an overflow of spirits that comes from feeling good not about yourself but about God."[8] It is in part a matter of perspective. We have hope that God will eventually get us out of a desperate situation, and, in that hope, there are the seeds of joy. "May those who sow in tears reap with shouts of joy."[9] All suffering, all pain, all emptiness, all disappointment is *seed*: sow it in God. He will, finally, bring a crop of joy from it.[10]

PRAYER: Dear Lord, I am going through a difficult time, and it is hard to see any joy in it. But let me learn from the apostle Paul, who says it is possible to "rejoice in our sufferings." Give me Your perspective on my problems, that in all things, You work for the good of those who love You. May You fill me with joy as I walk in faith with You. In Jesus' name, amen.

---

7   Eugene H. Peterson, *A Long Obedience in the Same Direction: Discipleship in an Instant Society* (Downers Grove, InterVarsity Press, 1980), 92.
8   Peterson, 96.
9   Peterson, 97; A quote from a Welsh hymn.
10 Peterson, 96.

16. THE IMPORTANCE OF CHURCH

1 John 1:7. *But if we walk in the light as he himself is in the light, we have fellowship with one another, and the blood of Jesus his Son cleanses us from all sin.*

It is my fervent hope that you are an active member of a church. It is so hard in these difficult times to "go it alone." And even though it is true that Christ often went off to be alone to meditate and pray and collect His thoughts, it is also true that after the church was established at Pentecost, the Bible does its work through the church. In fact, Eugene Peterson asserts, "The Bible knows nothing of a religion that is defined by what a person does inwardly in the privacy of thought or feeling, or apart from others in lonely retreat."[11] We benefit tremendously from the counsel, advice, and wisdom of our fellow believers. When we are going through a rough time, we can usually find someone in the church who can buoy us up. Of course, the church isn't perfect—people fall short and are at times hypocritical and may even come across as mean or uncaring. Their mean-ness merely indicates that those who are hurting are all the more in need of our love and encouragement. We aren't always one big happy family, but we are brothers and sisters in Christ. The relationships we form are our life line; the basis of community—"a place where each person is taken seriously, learns to trust others, depend on others, be compassionate with others, rejoice with others."[12]

PRAYER: Dear Lord, thank You for the church, a place that is much more than a building. It is filled with fellow believers, and through our personal relationships and acting as a community of believers, we can find help for our problems and a sense of peace and wellbeing for our lives. In Jesus' name, amen.

---

11   Eugene H. Peterson, *A Long Obedience in the Same Direction: Discipleship in an Instant Society* (Downers Grove, InterVarsity Press, 1980), 171.
12   Peterson, 174.

17. THE PRESENCE OF THE HOLY SPIRIT

Romans 8:26b. *We do not know how to pray as we ought, but that very Spirit intercedes with sighs too deep for words.*

Christians who are going through a difficult time have an invisible helper—the Holy Spirit. Catherine Marshall says that Jesus' presence in the Holy Spirit is actually better than having Him in person![13] He now resides *in* us and is constantly available, rather than the limited time we would get to spend with Him if He were here physically. Marshall goes on to say that many people don't sense the presence of the Holy Spirit in their lives. We can't give ourselves an exam to see if we "have" the Holy Spirit. The Holy Spirit comes at God's initiative and not ours. God sheds the light. Psalm 36:9b says "in your light we see light." How then are we to know whether the Holy Spirit resides in us? By seeking first God's righteousness. We read Scripture and are inspired by the Holy Spirit to see how these ancient words are speaking to us here and now. And we talk to other Christians so that through their helpful insight and wisdom we can discern things that would otherwise be hidden to us. Lastly, we take God at His word. When Jesus spoke to His disciples at the last supper, He promised that He would send us the Holy Spirit: "But the Advocate, the Holy Spirit, whom the Father will send in my name, will teach you everything, and remind you of all that I have said to you" (John 14:26). This is not a conditional promise. It is one made to all who are in Christ. The glimpses we have of the Holy Spirit's presence may be fleeting, or they may be very real and constant in your life, but they are there. Rest assured that as Christians, we have a great and wonderful Counselor who loves us, guides us, and is available to us.

PRAYER: Dear Lord, Thank You for the gift of the Holy Spirit. Although I cannot command answers from Him, or even in my own power know of His presence, I have faith that He is helping me along life's journey. Help me to find Him in your Word and in the counsel of other Christians. In Jesus' name, amen.

---

13   Catherine Marshall, *The Helper* (Grand Rapids, Chosen Books, 2001), 20.

18. FORGETTING YOUR DIFFICULT TIMES

John 14:21. *They who have my commandments and keep them are those who love me; and those who love me will be loved by my Father, and I will love them and reveal myself to them.*

The best way I know of forgetting about your own difficult times is to serve others. Serve a meal in a soup kitchen, build a Habitat for Humanity house, join a church committee or serve in a local volunteer organization or board. Preoccupation with serving others who are less fortunate than you is a surefire way to put things in proper perspective. There are many people in less fortunate situations than you and serving them puts your circumstances in a more favorable light. In service, we are modeling Christ's behavior. He sided with the poor, the sick, and the downtrodden and served them through His ministry of healing and words of consolation. Patrick Morley says, "It is by taking the narrow road of giving [service], that we end up in the broad road of receiving."[14] Christ loves those who serve Him and multiplies their blessings several fold over what they have given. "If you keep my commandments [and serve], you will abide in my love, just as I have kept my Father's commandments and abide in his love. I have said these things to you so that my joy may be in you, and that your joy may be complete" (John 15:10-11). Morley concludes, "In every place Jesus might visit today, he would want to know 'Where is the sting of the lack of the gospel felt in this place?'"[15] Most often those places are where people are hurting and in need. And then Jesus would go there to minister and serve. Will you?

PRAYER: Dear Lord, help me to serve others who are in need, and, in so doing, receive healing myself for my problems. Your life here on earth was a model of service, and I want to emulate it so that You are pleased with me, and I receive Your complete joy. In Jesus' name, amen.

---

14 Patrick Morley, *Ten Secrets for the Man in the Mirror* (Grand Rapids: Zondervan, 2000), 130.
15 Morley, 161.

19. THE KINGDOM IS IN YOUR MIDST[16]

John 15:16a. *You did not choose me but I chose you.*

The Kingdom of God is in our midst, but not to be fully grasped. We can't "own" the Kingdom personally; that is, we can't pretend that we are in control of God any more than we can fully define God and put Him in a box. "[The kingdom] is always an invitation, just enough to draw us deeper. Just enough of God to make us want more of God, but God is always in the driver's seat. 'You have not chosen me, I am always choosing you'" (John 15:16).[17] So during the frustration of your difficult time, remember that it is by design. God is a mystery and the way that your life unfolds is not predictable. But if we are willing to live with a certain amount of uncertainty in our lives, God will draw us deeper. We will grow. After all, we are co-creators in this wonderful process called "life." God has given us unique talents that can be used in partnership with Him to further His Kingdom. And our role is to accept the invitation of the Kingdom and marvel at the incredible opportunities that are before us. God opens doors, and rather than take them for granted, we need to enter into the fullness of His Kingdom. In your difficult time, look for glimpses of the Kingdom. It may come in the hug of a loved one, or something said by a complete stranger. Just look. The Kingdom is in your midst.

PRAYER: Dear Lord, Sometimes I have trouble seeing Your Kingdom in the middle of all my difficulties. But, it is in my midst. Help me to look around and see the ways that You are active in my world. We see as through a glass but dimly (1 Corinthians 13:12), but what we see is enough to spur us on. I can't fully know the Kingdom any more than I can fully know You in this life, but the glimpses I have are sufficient. Thank You for Your gift of love. In Jesus' name, amen.

---

16 Richard Rohr, *Preparing for Christmas: Daily Meditations for Advent* (Cincinnati: St. Anthony Messenger Press, 2008), 46-49; Portions paraphrased.
17 Rohr, 47.

20. CENTERING PRAYER

Matthew 6:6. *But whenever you pray, go into your room and shut the door and pray to your Father who is in secret; and your Father who sees in secret will reward you.*

If you are unsatisfied with your meditation/devotion time, and it is not providing relief for your difficult time, you might try a method that I have found helpful called "centering prayer." It was developed in the mid 1970's by Friar Thomas Keating, based on the contemplative practices of monks in the 16th century. Keating's popular book, *Open Mind, Open Heart* describes the method more fully. Basically, you calmly sit upright in a chair with your eyes closed, offer a brief prayer to God to recognize this special time of communing with God in one of His favorite ways, through silence, and then offer your own silence to Him in faith. When thoughts begin to enter your mind, as they invariably will, softly say the sacred word, a one or two syllable word that you have selected in advance (like Lord, Jesus, Abba, love, peace, etc.). Spend twenty minutes twice a day in this way (set a silent timer), and, over time, you will experience life in new and better ways. It is like going from seeing the world in black and white to full 3D color! At first, it will be difficult. Your mind will wander and be distracted by all sorts of things, and you will think that the 20 minutes will never be over. But as you get comfortable with the method, it will become a more and more natural part of your contemplative experience. Centering prayer is an exercise in effortlessness, of letting go, like taking the stopper out of a bathtub: the water goes down by itself, not needing to be pushed out. Remember, it isn't "bad" to have thoughts during centering prayer, just don't latch on to them or elaborate on them. Release them by saying the sacred word ever so gently. You should commit to this method at least for one month to see if it will work for you. You will be glad that you tried it.

PRAYER: Dear Lord, I know that You cherish silent times, and, through the practice of centering prayer, I can commune with You through our silence together. Thank You for making me aware of this method and help me to have the patience to try it for a month to see if it is mutually beneficial. In Jesus' name, amen.

21. THE RIGHT WAY TO BE HUMBLE

Ephesians 4:2. *With all humility and gentleness, with patience, bearing with one another in love.*

Humility is a virtue practiced by Christianity that is often misunderstood. Chuck Swindoll has some interesting "takes" on humility. Many people equate a humble person to a weak person, one who has a "milk toast" attitude and is easily pushed around. Nothing could be further from the truth. True, a humble person has a degree of meekness, but this is only in the recognition of how powerful and sovereign our God is: "The fear of the Lord is the beginning of wisdom" (Psalm 111:10). We have an awesome respect for God and His magnificence. But, we are made in the image of God and receive power in our own right—the power to serve God. It is this contrast between our God-given power and our humble attitude before God that makes the Christian so unique. In our sin, we take this "power trip" to heart and act as though it came from us alone. In our humility, we recognize that we are children of God and have our being because of His love and abundant grace toward us. No wonder that some people are so dismayed with Christian behavior and think that we are nothing but hypocrites. We are displaying the "power side" of our being and forgetting God's role in our lives. The Christian who "has it all together" is the one who uses his power in God's service and pays due homage to the source of his power: he is humble. At times, God disciplines us when we forget who is in charge. More often than not, we pay more attention to God when we are going through a difficult time. In the good times, it is too easy to pretend that we created the good times and are responsible for them. Humbling ourselves before God in the good times and the bad is a sign that we understand God's provision for our lives. So, walk in humility. It is not a sign of weakness. It shows that we are in a right relationship to our God.

PRAYER: Dear Lord, Help me to be humble. Not because I am weak or inadequate, but because it is a sign that I am in a right relationship with You. Thank You for all the gifts You have bestowed upon me, and for making me in Your image. In Jesus' name, amen.

22. WE CAN BECOME DISCIPLES[18]

Luke 14:26. *Whoever comes to me and does not hate father and mother, wife and children, brothers and sisters, yes, and even life itself, cannot be my disciple.*

What does it mean to be a disciple of Christ? I think that many people are content with the "followership" aspect of discipleship but don't count the cost of following Christ and don't recognize their leadership responsibilities. Christ did not fall into the mold of formal religion; He had radical thoughts for His day (and for all of time) and opposed a lot of "traditional" religious practices (especially those of the Pharisees). How did He train His disciples? By spending time with them. He chose a motley band of twelve, many of them going through difficult times of their own, and then loved them in such a way that they learned from Him and ultimately became able to carry His message after Christ left them. Charles Swindoll says, "During [the disciples'] years with him, truth had been carefully transferred, deep convictions replaced superficial beliefs, and a growing consecration and commitment to the eternal dimension emerged slowly yet firmly."[19] We too, can become disciples by immersing ourselves in Jesus' words (the Bible), praying for insight, and trusting in faith that we will grow to know Him more fully. This is not an easy endeavor. Read Luke 14:25-33 to see some of Christ's expectations for His disciples. In order to follow Him we must hate our wife and children and brothers and sisters and become part of a new family: Christ's family (of which our wife and children and brothers and sisters very much play a loving part). Swindoll asserts that there is no question of where our ultimate loyalty lies—disciples have no higher priority on their lives than Christ—not even their love for their own family members. Jesus says that we must carry our cross; be willing to take on the burdens, problems and toils of life in order to pursue Him fully. He says we must give up all our possessions—if there is any material thing that has a grip on our heart—let it go! We are to count the cost before we embark on any endeavor, like any prudent man would do before taking on a huge project like building a house. Jesus is the One who

18 Charles R. Swindoll, *Strengthening Your Grip: How to Live Confidently in an Aimless World* (Nashville, Thomas Nelson, 2003), 113; Portions paraphrased.
19 Swindoll, 113.

has counted the cost and selected the ones that He wants to go into battle with—His disciples! Do you begin to see what it means to be a disciple of Christ? It is not an easy task, but it is the most worthwhile one we can pursue.

PRAYER: Dear Lord, Help me to be Your disciple. I have counted the cost, and I am prepared to sacrifice all my attachments to this world to serve You. I thank You that I can spend time with You by reading Your Word and through prayer. Please convict me through the power of the Holy Spirit not only to follow You, but also to serve others and to have Kingdom priorities while I am here in this earth. In Jesus' name, amen.

23. GOD'S WORK VS. THE DEVIL'S WORK

Romans 8:39. *Nor height nor depth nor anything else in all creation, will be able to separate us from the love of God in Christ Jesus our Lord.*

Eugene Peterson asserts that the opposite of God's work is the devil's work, or, if you prefer, the work of this world's "powers and principalities." What is the main difference between God's work and the devil's? God works in very personal ways and always for our good. The devil works in impersonal ways and always for a result that furthers his own interest. Peterson says, "Every time that we embrace ways other than the ways of Jesus; try to manipulate people or events in ways that short-circuit personal relationships and intimacies, we are doing the devil's work."[20] We do the devil's work when we reduce every man or woman to a function rather than a person, and we become so focused on the result that we trample over other people to get it done. We know that people (including you!) have problems and shortcomings and we must make allowances for peoples' prejudices, egotism, ambition, superstition, ignorance, greed, and avarice. We do this by loving them despite their shortcomings, and at the opportune time discussing their issues in a loving way so that we are in a right relationship to them and God and can work together for the ultimate good of a project. This is "deep and full" living, not just pleasure-seeking, blind to the marvels of nature, but appreciative of the time and talents (and shortcomings) of those we love. Peterson says, "For all our capacity to meet needs, we have an astonishing capacity for not noticing the needs of people we don't like or who will overly inconvenience us."[21] Pay attention to this form of selective "do-goodism." It is rampant in the United States, where Americans are known for being selective in who they serve and how they serve them—whatever makes us look the best. Try to overcome your difficult time by mimicking the way Jesus served and loved—unconditionally, with no thought of reward. You will begin to experience the kind of Kingdom life that Jesus promises. You will experience it here and now, and not have to wait.

---

20 Eugene H. Peterson, *The Jesus Way: A Conversation on the Ways That Jesus Is the Way* (Grand Rapids: Wm. B. Eerdmans, 2007), 36.
21 Peterson, 31.

PRAYER: Dear Lord, Thank You for being the Holy One in our lives who can do only good. Forgive us when we treat others impersonally and become focused only on the result. Help us to mimic Your unconditional love for others so that we can live with Kingdom priorities here and now. In Jesus' name, amen.

24. JESUS IS THE WORD

John 5:19. Jesus said to them, "Very truly, I tell you, the Son can do nothing on his own, but only what he sees the Father doing; for whatever the Father does, the Son does likewise."

A professor of Presbyterian University, Peter Hobbe, of Clinton, South Carolina, visited our church one Sunday and gave a wonderful insight of the Word of God. We recognize that Scripture is God's Word for us; given to us for "teaching, for reproof, for correction, and for training in righteousness" (2 Timothy 3:16). But, we also realize that Jesus is indeed the Word of God. John 1:1 says, "In the beginning was the Word [Jesus], and the Word was with God, and the Word was God." So, when reading Scripture, we should always do it through the lens and perspective of Jesus. Jesus describes Himself as "gentle and humble in heart" (Matthew 11:29). So, the lens through which we see the Scripture is through that of humility, not of power, prestige, or possessions. Much of the Old Testament readings deal with human struggles with power, prestige, and possessions, and there are frequent wars, trials, and tribulations that confront Old Testament people. Often, these war-like and power mongering attributes are ascribed to God. But, when seen through the lens of Jesus, who is unconditional love, we put the text in perspective—it is man's tendency toward evil doing that is at fault here, not God. What a comfort it is to have the living God acting in our lives here and now through the Holy Spirit, giving us the Truth about what Jesus would do if He were here with us. Scripture provides a wealth of insight and wisdom and Jesus provides the perspective that we need to overcome our struggles and strengthen our faith. I don't know about you, but the Bible gives me comfort precisely because people struggle and rebel against God, just like you and me. Benefit from those scriptural examples and take comfort that if God is present in their circumstances, He is present in yours, because He loves you.

PRAYER: Dear God, thank You for Jesus, our Lord and Savior who is the ultimate Word and who guides our thoughts and actions. When we think about what You would do in a certain circumstance, we just need to ask whether Jesus would have done it and know in our hearts what is the right thing to do. In Jesus' name, amen.

25. SUFFERING IS WORTH THE PRICE

Romans 8:20-21. *For the creation was subjected to futility, not of its own will but by the will of the one who subjected it, in hope that the creation itself will be set free from its bondage to decay and will obtain the freedom of the glory of the children of God.*

You have turned to these reflections because you are going through a difficult time and don't know how to cope with it. No one fully understands why we must suffer, but it is part of the Christian experience here on earth, and no one is immune from it. Part of the reason is explained by Patrick Morley, "God makes every avenue that leads away from him into a dead end. Apart from him, life has no meaning. Futility is the chief tool God uses to sovereignly draw men to himself of their own free will."[22] That still may not be much comfort. I like the pruning analogy that the disciple John uses, "every branch that bears fruit he prunes to make it bear more fruit" (John 15:2). The disciples realized that suffering was worth the price: "I consider that the sufferings of this present time are not worth comparing with the glory about to be revealed to us" (Romans 8:18). Still not satisfied? Then consider how Morley concludes his chapter on suffering. "An old black woman in the Deep South put suffering in proper perspective when she said, 'If the mountain was smooth, you couldn't climb it' . . . your sufferings are not merely setbacks. They are also springboards to the crucial task of knowing God well enough that you can trust him. We must learn to interpret the mysteries of life in the light of our knowledge of God. Until we can look the darkest fact full in the face without damaging God's character, we do not yet know him as he is."[23]

PRAYER: Dear Lord, Have mercy on me and ease my suffering. But in the meantime, help me to recognize that You are pruning me for a better time, including that grand and glorious time when I am united with You in heaven. In Jesus' name, amen.

---

22   Patrick Morley, *Ten Secrets for the Man in the Mirror* (Grand Rapids: Zondervan, 2000), 68.
23   Morley, 72.

26. PEOPLE ARE AT THE CENTER OF OUR WORK

Exodus 39:42-43. *The Israelites had done all the work just as the Lord had commanded Moses. When Moses saw that they had done all the work just as the Lord had commanded, he blessed them.*

What is your attitude towards work? A "necessary evil," something you do to get by in the world, to distract you from your difficult time, or is it a source of satisfaction in your life? Eugene Peterson asserts that work is a good and necessary aspect of our lives. God worked to create the heavens and the earth, and He declared it good (Genesis 1). We need to develop a balanced perspective about our work; neither the "workaholic" approach, where work is everything, nor the lethargic approach, where work is boring and to be "avoided at all costs" are healthy. Seen in its proper perspective, we begin to realize that *people* are at the center of Christian work. When we invest our energy into the people we work for and with, we become less consumer driven. We change our attitude from work as a source to *get* things, to work as a way of being in creative relationship with one another. A pastor in my church once said, "Perhaps in the long run, we will be remembered not so much for what we did, as for who we did it with." After all, the people we work with are eternal beings, versus the goods and services we produce that will rust away or be moth-eaten. Of course, that is not to say that the things we produce are not important. God gives them to us here and now for our enjoyment, and He likes nothing better than when we are using our time and talents in the creative process. It is especially pleasing to Him when we put our work or volunteer efforts toward an act of love and justice, or helping and healing, or liberating and cheering. Is one of the sources of your difficult times related to work (or the lack thereof)? Pray about it. Reflect on orienting your work to the glory of God. No matter how menial the task, when we turn it over to God, it has meaning. A famous monk, John of the Cross, spent most of his time washing the dishes for the monastery, but he used that time to reflect on God's goodness, and he was content in his dish washing. When we keep

God in the center of our lives, when we work with dignity and purpose, God is pleased, and we are fulfilled.

PRAYER: Dear Lord, You worked in the creation of heaven and the earth and found it to be good. Help us to see value in our work, no matter how insignificant the task may seem. Help us to see value not only in the goods and services we produce, but in the relationships with our co-workers and bosses, who are created in Your image and are so important to Your Kingdom. In Jesus' name, amen.

27. MOVING FROM THINGS "I SHOULD DO" TO THINGS "I LIKE TO DO"[24]

Psalm 34:8a. *O taste and see that the LORD is good.*

There are things that you "should" or "ought" to do, and things that you like to do. Spiritual growth is moving your relationship with God from the "I should" to the "I like" list. Some things are like drudgery to do: paying taxes, doing laundry, cleaning your room. But if you put going to church and praying and practicing the spiritual disciplines in the same category, then you've got some work to do. God wants you to like Him. God wants you to take pleasure in relating to Him and thinking about Him. In fact, God plants desires in our hearts. Many of these desires are for worldly things like money and clothes and achievement and looking attractive and having friends. And there is nothing wrong with these desires, if they don't become objects of worship. But along with those worldly desires comes a desire for God—to know Him better and be in right relationship with Him. "Spiritual growth doesn't mean a life of doing what I *should* do instead of what I want to do. It means coming to want to do what I should do. . . . when people come to understand how good God is, they want him. They don't just love him. They *like* him."[25] Psalm 34:8 says, "O taste and see that the LORD is good." Tasting is pleasurable—something we like to do. Try a sample; enjoy it; eat more. That is how it is to be with our spiritual life. Thoughts of unworthiness, overriding concern about sin, overly obsessing about your difficult time, fear of God's judgment—all these concerns should not deter us from the delight and joy that we take in knowing God and getting to know Him better.

PRAYER: Dear Lord, Help me to see the exercise of my spiritual disciplines not as a chore but as a delight—something I want to do rather than ought to do. You are a God of love who instills in me desires—desires to enjoy the things of this world and to enjoy the spiritual things that I can't yet fully see but are just as real. Thank You for the gift of the Holy Spirit, who gives me glimpses into the Kingdom of God. In Jesus' name, amen.

---

24 John Ortberg, *The Me I Want To Be: Becoming God's Best Version of You* (Grand Rapids: Zondervan, 2009), 79-81; Portions paraphrased.
25 Ortberg, 81.

28. PRESS ON

Philippians 3:14. *I press on toward the goal for the prize of the heavenly call of God in Christ Jesus.*

"If at first you don't succeed, try, try again." There is a lot to be said about perseverance, especially during difficult times. Too often, we give up or become disheartened after one or two attempts at something. Consider the parable of the widow before the judge (Luke 18:1-8). What if she had quit after one request? My father was a model of perseverance. Once, my mother broke a valuable vase into several pieces, and my father painstakingly fit and glued all the pieces back together until you could barely tell that it had been broken. It took him multiple attempts. After he completed the work, I sent him these encouraging words from Chuck Swindoll, "Press on. Nothing in the world can take the place of persistence. Talent will not. Nothing is more common than unsuccessful men with talent. Genius will not. Unrewarded genius is almost a proverb. Education will not. The world is full of educated derelicts. Persistence and determination alone are important."[26] Are you discouraged in an unproductive job search? Press on. Are you struggling to relate and apply the appropriate level of discipline to children in their difficult teenage years? Press on. No matter what the difficulty you face, if you persevere, you will ultimately be rewarded. The way of faith requires perseverance and has precedent: the Jews faced exile, Jesus and later Paul and the other apostles suffered. But they all persevered— they all "[pressed] on toward the goal for the prize of the heavenly call of God in Christ Jesus" (Philippians 3:14).

Eugene Peterson highlights an important point: "Perseverance does not mean to be "perfect." It means that we keep going. We do not quit when we find that we are not yet mature and that there is a long journey still before us."[27] We may get angry, we may get frustrated, we may display any number of human emotions that show that we care and have a sense of urgency. Nor is perseverance resignation or being "stuck in a rut." We must try all variety

---

26   Charles Swindoll. *Persistence,* radio, 1987.
27   Eugene H. Peterson, *A Long Obedience in the Same Direction: Discipleship in an Instant Society* (Downers Grove: InterVarsity Press, 1980), 127.

of things to overcome our difficulty. Be creative about it. Use your God given talents. Persevere.

PRAYER: Dear Lord, Help me to persevere in all that I do. Even when I get angry or frustrated, it just means that I care passionately about life. I just need to "stay the course," and I can do it only with Your help. In Jesus' name, amen.

29. WE ARE NOT IMMUNE
FROM SUFFERING

Psalm 119:153. *Look on my misery and rescue me, for I do not forget your law.*

Perhaps your difficult time is due to some type of suffering, maybe a physical ailment or mental anguish. Certainly, we know from experience that the Christian is not immune to suffering. Christ suffered for us on the cross, and the disciples and early Christians were subjected to persecution and imprisonment. What makes us any different? When we try to act as though there should be no suffering, to ignore it or set it aside, we devalue the experience of suffering. Suffering is reality; it is part of the human condition. In fact, as Christians, we are at the heart of things when we suffer—we are perhaps closer to God than at any other time of our life. I suffered greatly when I went through my cancer treatments, and yet it was a time of intense spiritual growth and strengthening of family and church ties. I prayed the Psalms every night; I relied on church members to take me to my chemo treatments and had many insightful exchanges with them; my wife was like a rock and my lifeline, and my children became even more precious. Yes, we enter the depths, but with the realization that "God is deeper than the deepest depth in man."[28] He has been there in Christ and knows every detail of our suffering. What we do when we suffer is to wait and hope. While we wait, as much as possible, we go about our assigned tasks, confident that God will provide the meaning and conclusions.[29] And, we hope. Our hope is in Christ, our source of strength and our personal Redeemer. We have faith that at some point our suffering will be over, whether in this life or certainly in the next, only God knows. No matter how deep the pain, God is deeper, and "underneath are the everlasting arms" (Deuteronomy 33:27 KJV). So be patient, be faithful, have hope, draw close to God. He is there, especially during your time of suffering.

PRAYER: Dear Lord, Help me to endure this time of suffering with Your help. Draw me close to You and hold me tight. Help me to keep in perspective Your glorious plan, knowing that this time of suffering will pass, and a new day will dawn, and I will be stronger for what I have gone through. In Jesus' name, amen.

---

28 Eugene H. Peterson, *A Long Obedience in the Same Direction: Discipleship in an Instant Society* (Downers Grove: InterVarsity Press, 1980), 134.
29 Peterson, 139.

30. BE A PERSON OF ASPIRATION

Matthew 18:4. *Whoever becomes humble like this child is the greatest in the kingdom of heaven.*

We talked earlier of humility (Reflection 21) and how important it is for a Christian to have a humble attitude. Eugene Peterson provides some wonderful insight in humility in Chapter 13 of his book *A Long Obedience in the Same Direction*.[30] The image is that of a weaned child, resting at his mother's breast; calm and comforted—content and not seeking his own ambition. This is quite a contrast to our current culture, which places a premium on ambition. Ambition, the basic sin of taking things into your own hands, being your own God, grabbing what there is while you can get it, is now regarded as a basic wisdom. But, on the flip side, humility doesn't mean that we are doormats either, the person who is used by others to clean up the mess of everyday living and then discarded. Instead, be a person of aspiration in order to help overcome your difficult time. Keep God in the equation and recognize God as the source of our energy and creativity. But, don't *use* God as though He will grant your every wish just as you want. Instead, develop a childlike trust in God, just like the image we portrayed above of the child weaned and gently resting at his mother's side—loving her for her own sake, and *not* for the gratification she can bring. The mature, weaned child recognizes that his mother is his source of comfort even though she may at times deny him comfort. Our relationship to God should be like that—we desire God for ourselves, but not just as a way of fulfilling our wishes—we rest in God. And we have really matured in our walk with God when we can forgo the joys which once appeared to be essential; when we can "weather through" the difficult times and can still find our solace in Him who denies them to us.

PRAYER: Dear Lord, I know that I can't always have it my way. Help me to trust that You have a plan for my life, and, in humility, let me rest at Your side like a child who has been weaned from his mother and loves her for who she is, not what she can do for him. In Jesus' name, amen.

---

30 Eugene H. Peterson, *A Long Obedience in the Same Direction: Discipleship in an Instant Society* (Downers Grove: InterVarsity Press, 1980), 143-154.

31. FAITH AND DOUBT

John 20:25b. *But [Thomas] said to them (the disciples), "Unless I see the mark of the nails in his hands, and put my finger in the mark of the nails and my hand in his side, I will not believe."*

One thing I am pretty sure that you have experienced is periods of doubt in your life, probably accentuated in your difficult time. Is there really such a thing as eternal life? Are the promises of Jesus true? It is normal to experience times of both faith and doubt. Often, we think that the opposite of faith is doubt, but, actually, the opposite of faith is *certainty*. If we were absolutely certain of everything, there wouldn't be need for faith—we would know everything and have God all figured out. But, God is much larger than that and much more mysterious. John Ortberg says that both faith and doubt are part of our lives[31]: "Doubt is not so much a dividing line that separates people into different camps as it is a razor's edge that runs through every soul."[32] We are overwhelmed with faith and excitement when we hold a newborn baby; we are overcome with doubt when a little, helpless baby dies. There are things about God that we just don't understand, many of which we've discussed in these reflections. Why does He allow suffering and pain and death? So, doubt is a normal part of our life—it just means that we don't have all the answers and need to keep on seeking them and praying about them. "Believing and doubting share the same inevitability, but they are not equal. They cannot lay the same claim on our allegiance. They do not share the same power. If there are places beyond [this world], doubt cannot take you there."[33]

PRAYER: Dear Lord, Sometimes I experience times of doubt. As Mark 9:24 says, "I believe; help my unbelief!" My doubt is a condition where I admit that I don't understand it all, just as my faith is witness to the fact that I don't understand it all. Thank You for the Holy Spirit that helps to convince me that Your word is true, and my periods of doubt are temporary. In Jesus' name, amen.

---

31 John Ortberg, *Faith and Doubt* (Grand Rapids: Zondervan, 2008).
32 Ortberg, 23; Quoting writer, Michael Novak.
33 Ortberg, 26.

32. STEWARDSHIP

1 Corinthians 7:7b. *Each has a particular gift from God, one having one kind and another a different kind.*

Let's talk a bit about stewardship. Your antenna goes up and you say, "Oh no, here comes another lesson about tithing." But, stewardship is more than money. It is an attitude about life which, when practiced, can help us put things in proper perspective and even make some of our difficult times less bothersome. According to Patrick Morley, "Stewardship is a total way of looking at life which understands that everything comes from God, belongs to God, and is to be used for the glory of God."[34] Morley asserts that the faithful steward comes to realize that he is managing God's gifts—he doesn't own them. He is happy with what he gets; he doesn't link happiness to getting what he wants. He sees life as a process and is less concerned with the result. He recognizes that God produces fruit through him; not that he on his own must produce fruit to please God. Do you begin to see the proper attitude of a steward and how releasing it is? That is not to say that we are "off the hook" when it comes to the traditional concept of tithing, but our attitude is that we are just giving back to God a portion of what He has already given us; not that we are reluctantly tearing off a piece of what we own. This recognition of God's sovereignty is a tremendous help to the individual soul. Morley says, "A steward knows that he has enough time to complete every task God intends him to do. A steward does not have to worry about the future because he knows that God is not only good but is sovereignly in control. A steward knows that God will not fail to complete the good work— the 'plan'—he has begun."[35]

PRAYER: Dear Lord, thank You for giving me a more complete picture of what stewardship is all about. Help me to trust that You have a plan for my life, and that everything I own is a gift from You. Help me to be an effective manager of the gifts, talents, and resources You have given me. In Jesus' name, amen.

---

34 Patrick Morley, *Ten Secrets for the Man in the Mirror* (Grand Rapids: Zondervan, 2000), 99.
35 Morley, 99.

33. WHAT TO DO AFTER YOU HAVE "ARRIVED"

2 Corinthians 5:9. *So whether we are at home or away, we make it our aim to please him.*

Perhaps your difficulty is that you have achieved a long sought-after goal and are still dissatisfied. You thought, "If I can only achieve [insert your favorite goal here], then I will be complete and can sit back and relax" (and bask in the glory of my accomplishment). If the goal is a material or physical one and does not credit God's role in getting you there, it will not bring the intended level of satisfaction. So, what does one do when he has "arrived"? You bless the Lord. What does that look like? Erick Routley thinks that, colloquially, "to bless" means "to speak well of."[36] The Lord has spoken well of you in helping you reach your goal, now you are to speak well of Him. It enhances your accomplishment. It gives it an added dimension. It will prevent you from saying, "Is that all there is?"[37] Maybe you don't feel like blessing the Lord. Eugene Peterson provides the answer: "Go through the motions of blessing God and your spirit will pick up the cue and follow along . . . act your gratitude; pantomime your thanks; you will become that which you do."[38] You may think that you have to change the way you feel before you can be thankful, but feelings are tricky things to control. It is far better to act out your praise and drag your feelings out of the doldrums along with it. You may be pleasantly surprised when you try this concept. "Feelings don't run the show. There is a reality deeper than our feelings. Live by that."[39] What is that reality? The reality that God is in charge; that God has a plan for your life; that God loves you unconditionally. Come to grips with that and you will realize the chief end of man: "To glorify God and enjoy him forever."[40]

---

36 Eugene H. Peterson, *A Long Obedience in the Same Direction: Discipleship in an Instant Society* (Downers Grove: InterVarsity Press, 1980); As referenced by the author.

37 Peggy Lee. "Is That All There Is?" Recorded 2001. Track 12 on *A Natural Woman.* Vinyl; Portrays well the feeling of going through life, reaching a milestone, and then being depressed about it.

38 Peterson, 188.

39 Peterson, 189.

40 The first question in the Westminster Shorter Catechism.

PRAYER: Dear Lord, No wonder I don't feel satisfied when I reach a goal. I haven't given You credit for it! Help me to speak well of You, to bless You, when I accomplish something, or even when I fall short! And if I don't feel like it, let me bless You anyway, and in so doing, come to the wonderful realization that You love me unconditionally, and have a plan for me. In Jesus' name, amen.

34. ABOUT ANXIETY[41]

Philippians 4:6. *Do not worry about anything, but in everything by prayer and supplication with thanksgiving let your requests be made known to God.*

"Prayer is the single most fundamental spiritual discipline when it comes to putting off anxiety and putting on peace."[42] Even though the Bible tells us not to be anxious, it is wired into our framework to be so. Some people are more troubled than others, but we all have experienced those times of worry that we can't seem to shake. Likely, you are distressed right now, in your difficult time. Trying to tell ourselves not to worry just seems to make us even more concerned. Jesus was a calming presence, and He sent the Holy Spirit to be the peaceful presence for all of us. That is why prayer is so important to reducing our fears and concerns. It connects us to a non-anxious presence. When we were little, our parents served that function. We could hug our mom tightly when we got frightened. We no longer have mom's shelter, but we have the equivalent in Jesus. "We have a settled conviction that goes down to the core of our being—to our belly where rivers of living water can flow—that all things are in God's hands. Therefore, all things will be well, and we can live free of worry, burden and fear."[43] Another thing that helps is to never worry alone. Seek out a friend to share your worries with and he will be a sounding board and likely be able to assuage your fear. One more thing which is sometimes hard to enact: we need to *do* the things we are afraid of! If we put them off, or shove them out of our consciousness, they will only come back later to bite us. Putting off speaking in front of a crowd or confronting the boss about an injustice will only delay the inevitable, and in the meantime, you will have worried in vain. Remember, "love casts out fear" (1 John 4:18), so hold fast to God's love and spread God's love to others, and there will be little room for fear.

---

41 John Ortberg, *The Me I Want To Be: Becoming God's Best Version of You* (Grand Rapids: Zondervan, 2009), 116-125; Portions paraphrased.
42 Ortberg, 124.
43 Ortberg, 117.

PRAYER: Dear Lord, I admit that I am frequently anxious and sometimes can't seem to get a handle on why. In those times, help me to find comfort in Your presence through praying, reading Scripture, and seeking the advice of other Christians. I know that You love me and that "love casts out fear" (1 John 4:18). Also, when I procrastinate about doing a task because I am fearful of it, help me to do it so that I can get my fear behind me and, through practice, get comfortable with the thing that I dread. In Jesus' name, amen.

35. ABSORB THE SUFFERING[44]

2 Corinthians 1:6. If we are being afflicted, it is for your consolation and salvation; if we are being consoled, it is for your consolation, which you experience when you patiently endure the same sufferings that we are also suffering.

There is an aspect of suffering that is easy to overlook: we tend to pass on our suffering to others in a "poor me, have pity on me (shouldn't this be you instead of me)" attitude. Or, perhaps we are angry at another person for the perception that he or she is causing our suffering and seek some way to pay them back. Jesus didn't do that. He received our hatred and didn't return it. "He does not first look at changing others, but pays the price of change within himself. He absorbs the mystery of human sin rather than passing it on. He does not use His suffering and death as power over others to punish them, but as power for others to transform them. He became the crucified so we would stop crucifying."[45] We are prone to mobilize for vengeance (while sometimes calling it "justice"), or looking for someone to blame, or someone to sue! Instead, we need to learn to absorb the suffering (the "Paschal Mystery"). We don't understand why it must occur; just that it is part of God's way for us to fully appreciate Him. But the key is to take it in; don't pass it on. Think of it as a "sacred wound," the transforming moment. As Richard Rohr says, "The wounded one is always the one with the gift, the comfortable one knows nothing."[46] We grow from our suffering, perhaps more fully than in any other way.

PRAYER: Dear Lord, I recognize my tendency to blame others for my suffering and difficult time. Instead, Your example says to take it in and not pass the blame. Suffering is part of Your plan for us. We don't understand it and wish there were some other way. Help us to accept it and be transformed by it. In Jesus' name, amen.

---

44 Richard Rohr, *Hope Against Darkness: The Transforming Vision of Saint Francis in an Age of Anxiety* (Cincinnati: St. Anthony Messenger Press, 2001), Kindle, 620-755. Portions paraphrased.
45 Rohr, 628, 755.
46 Rohr, 1115.

36. REFLECTING ON THE DAY

Psalm 48:9. *We ponder your steadfast love, O God, in the midst of your temple.*

I find a lot of comfort when I go to bed by thinking back upon the events of the day and trying to see how God was working in each event. It is a centuries-old tradition called "The Examen." Calmly think about your day as it unfolded and note the times where you sensed the presence of God. Do it in a prayerful manner, like you were conversing with God. As described by James Martin, SJ, the method goes like this: First, you approach God in gratitude, recalling anything in the day for which you are especially grateful, and giving thanks. Then, you review the events of the day in detail from start to finish, enumerating the details of your difficult time, noticing where you felt God's presence, and recognizing where you accepted or turned away from any invitations to grow in love. Third, you recall any actions for which you are sorry, which then leads to asking God for forgiveness and ends in grace, where you ask God for the grace you need for the next day and for the ability to see God's presence more clearly.[47] Perhaps your difficult time will be seen from a different perspective as you reflect on how it "played out" during the day. Maybe things weren't as daunting as you first perceived them; maybe you see in retrospect how God was guiding you or another person was helping you. Any form of prayer like this is a good way to help you through your difficult time.

PRAYER: Dear Lord, Help me to practice "The Examen" and to think about the wondrous encounters that I have had with You throughout my day that perhaps I didn't recognize or take the time to realize the significance of. Reflection is a good way to relive my day and realize my blessings and shortcomings and embrace Your grace. In Jesus' name, amen.

---

47   James Martin, SJ, *The Jesuit Guide to (Almost) Everything: A Spirituality for Real Life* (New York: HarperCollins, 2010), 97-98.

37. LIVING A SURRENDERED LIFE[48]

Jeremiah 29:11. *For surely I know the plans I have for you, says the LORD, plans for your welfare and not for harm, to give you a future with hope.*

You may consider your life a failure. Consider this: in human terms, *Jesus'* life was a failure! It ended in an ugly death on a cross with a humiliating sign over His head, "King of the Jews." He was abandoned by His disciples and felt forsaken by God. And then there was His liberating resurrection and the awakening of His disciples into agents of change which transformed the world! We can't always see the positive outcome of our perceived "failure." It is partly because we think that we know what our lives are meant to be, even though God has a different plan and outcome in mind. "Can you imagine being able to trust that the outcome of your efforts will be right, whatever the outcome? Even though it looks like every effort is marked with failure?"[49] That attitude is called leading a surrendered life. It doesn't mean that there is no effort—God expects a lot of effort on our part to strive for justice and peace in this world. And, you trust that your efforts are not in vain, no matter what the short-term outcome. The positive effect may not even occur until after your lifetime. Desmond Tutu tells story after story of people who were thwarted in their efforts to end apartheid in South Africa and could have fallen into despair were it not for their conviction that they were working for a just cause which would eventually prevail.[50] Some lost their lives before seeing an end to this unjust system, but they trusted that their efforts were not in vain. In your difficult time, try to see beyond your own solutions and surrender your life to God. It will lighten your load.

PRAYER: Dear Lord, Help me to lead a surrendered life. Too often, I want to control how things turn out, and I ignore Your sovereignty and the "big picture" of life. I pray for patience and perspective so that I am not frustrated with life but liberated to see that there is meaning to life even when things seem their darkest. In Jesus' name, amen.

---

48   Richard Rohr, *Hope Against Darkness: The Transforming Vision of Saint Francis in an Age of Anxiety* (Cincinnati: St. Anthony Messenger Press, 2001), Kindle 1315; Portions paraphrased.

49   Desmond Tutu, *Made for Goodness: And Why This Makes All the Difference* (New York: HarperOne, 2010), 120.

50   Read Tutu's book, *Made for Goodness,* for his inspirational stories of courage.

38. A SERVANT CHRISTIAN IS THE FREEST PERSON ON EARTH

Romans 1:9. *For God, whom I serve with my spirit by announcing the gospel of his Son, is my witness that without ceasing I remember you always in my prayers.*

One surefire way to lift yourself out of your depression, self-pity, and difficult time is to live a life of service. Eugene Peterson asserts, "I have never heard a servant Christian complain of the oppressiveness of the servitude. I have never yet heard a servant Christian rail against the restrictions of her service. A servant Christian is the freest person on earth."[51] But to serve others freely and without complaint, we must first look to God. God in Christ Jesus serves us. But that is not to say that He can be manipulated. Quite the opposite: "God did not become a servant so that we could order him around but so that we could join him in a redemptive lifestyle."[52] When we look to Jesus as our model of servitude and emulate His actions, we get it. The term for this is relying on God's mercy. "The word mercy means that the upward look to God in the heavens does not expect God to stay in the heavens, but to come down, to enter our condition, to accomplish the vast enterprise of redemption, to fashion in us, his eternal salvation."[53] God has a plan for us; He is fashioning us into His image, and part of the mold He is fashioning us into is that of a servant. "Love your neighbor as yourself" (Mark 12:31) is the operative command. Equipped with that kind of love and empowered by God, it is easier to develop a lifestyle of servanthood. "The Christian is a person who recognizes that our real problem is not in achieving freedom but in learning service under a better master."[54] And, do your service with a sense of urgency: don't wait around for God to direct you to service! There are crying needs out there begging for someone to help. You can be the one to help, and, in so doing, you will feel better about yourself and your situation.

PRAYER: Dear Lord, Thank You for the opportunity to serve You and my neighbor. Help me to become more aware of service opportunities and to act on them knowing that acts of service will help me every bit as much as the person being served.

---

51 Eugene H. Peterson, *A Long Obedience in the Same Direction: Discipleship in an Instant Society* (Downers Grove: InterVarsity Press, 1980), 64.
52 Peterson, 58.
53 Peterson, 60.
54 Peterson, 61.

39. NURTURING FRIENDSHIPS

1 Chronicles 12:17a. *David went out to meet them and said to them, "If you have come to me in friendship, to help me, then my heart will be knit to you.*

Having a good network of friends is a tremendous blessing. But, it takes work to gain a friend and keep a friend. James Martin, SJ, has some good suggestions for establishing and maintaining friendships.[55] First, you must be honest with each other. Friendships must be based on mutual trust that comes from complete transparency and honesty. Second, you must wish for the good of the other. No room for jealousy here or excessive competition. Give your friends the benefit of the doubt when questions arise and give them the freedom to pursue their own aspirations. Don't send them on a guilt trip if they sometimes can't spend as much time with you as you would like. They need to feel free to live their lives as well as enjoy your friendship. A little "friendly competition" is a good thing but not if it leads to wishing ill of the other person. Third, know when to be "discreetly silent." Sometimes friends need to puzzle things out on their own, and not be spoon fed with a solution that might work for you but be wrong for them. Just be there for them; let them know you are behind them all the way, but don't overdo it in the advice category. Fourth, give your friend the freedom to change. We all grow in different ways, and to hold back your friend so you can keep things like they always were between you is not healthy. Fifth, friendship is welcoming. Don't try to "hang on" to one friend exclusively at the expense of others. There is lots of room for friendships to flourish in a group setting, and it may be unhealthy to become too attached to just one person. I hope that these ideas for healthy friendships are helpful to you in your difficult time, and that you develop a wonderful network of good friends as a result.

PRAYER: Dear Lord, I cherish my friendships and want them to grow. Help me to take the lessons in this reflection to heart, so that I can maintain healthy relationships with my friends. In Jesus' name, amen.

---

55 James Martin, SJ, *The Jesuit Guide to (Almost) Everything: A Spirituality for Real Life* (New York: HarperCollins, 2010), 260-263.

40. YOU CANNOT LOSE YOUR FAITH[56]

1 Corinthians 10:13b. *God is faithful, and he will not let you be tested beyond your strength, but with the testing he will also provide the way out so that you may be able to endure it.*

How secure are you in your faith? Do you think that when you are at a low point and your faith ebbs that God thinks less of you? Think again! Eugene Peterson asserts that once you have professed your faith and claimed God's promises for yourself, you cannot lose it. Of course, God will not force you into His Kingdom. A pastor friend of mine said, "I am absolutely certain that God is not going to make someone go to heaven who doesn't want to be there." But, we're not talking about that person; we're talking about you and your concern that you might lose your salvation when you doubt or have periods when God seems distant from you. Don't worry. "Discipleship is not a contract in which if we break our part of the agreement, [God] is free to break his; it is a covenant in which he establishes the conditions and guarantees the results."[57] Relax. Rest secure in the covenant God has made with you. But, what if you are going through an extremely difficult time or illness and think that God has abandoned you? The trial is temporary. The apostle Paul tells us, "God is faithful, and he will not let you be tested beyond your strength, but with the testing he will also provide the way out so that you may be able to endure it" (1 Corinthians 10:13). If the trial and evil were permanent, without the hope of relief, no Christian could hold up under it. But, praise God! It is temporary. It may seem like a long time, but relief in some form or another will finally come for God's faithful. Stay the course. Try not to live by what you feel (depressed; moody), but by who God is (a Stronghold; Sovereign). "[Your] security comes from who God is, not from how [you] feel. Discipleship is a decision to live by what [you] know about God, not by what [you] feel about him or [yourself] or [your] neighbors."[58] In your difficult time, reflect on who God is and His promises, and you will begin to feel better.

---

56 Eugene H. Peterson, *A Long Obedience in the Same Direction: Discipleship in an Instant Society* (Downers Grove: InterVarsity Press, 1980), 83-85; Portions paraphrased.
57 Peterson, 85.
58 Peterson, 83.

PRAYER: Dear Lord, Even though I go through periods of doubt, I can rest assured that You still care for me and love me. My times of sickness or depression are only temporary. When I experience them, help me to get a handle on my feelings and think about You and Your strength and sovereignty instead so that I can rest in Your love and look forward to a better day. In Jesus' name, amen.

41. CHANGING THINGS FOR THE BETTER[59]

2 Samuel 14:19b-20a. *For it was your servant Joab who commanded me; it was he who put all these words into the mouth of your servant. In order to change the course of affairs your servant Joab did this.*

"The purpose of Christianity is not to critique or criticize this world in which we live. It is to *change* it."[60] How often do we get caught up in political arguments or societal relationship arguments and blame the other guy? It's so easy to do—fun even because it lets us off the hook. But, when we really examine ourselves, we find that there is little that we have done on our own right to change things for the better. A good example is the apostle Paul, who had every right to complain about the Romans and the difficult circumstances and roadblocks they put in front of his ministry. But, you never heard him complain about "the system." Instead, he pointed out his own sinfulness and went about his incredible missionary work despite all obstacles. We can change people's lives just by being faithful examples of God's grace in our lives. You'd be amazed at the positive statement you make just by living out your faith day by day. "Always preach the gospel, and when necessary, use words," is a poignant way of saying it.[61] Christians don't just sit back and wait for a message from God before they act. They recognize that God has given us a free will and creative talents to use on His behalf. Take comfort that your Christian walk is helping someone else, even though you yourself may be feeling down due to your difficult time. Sometimes, in our prayer life, we may find it easier to ask God to do all the work. If we really listen in on our prayers, God is saying, "Yes, I'm glad that you have come to Me in prayer and I recognize that Bill and Suzie (or whoever you are praying for) need My help, but they need your help, too." There is so much we can do to help change things rather than complain about them.

PRAYER: Dear Lord, Help me to be a good Christian example to the people around me. Keep me from complaining about my circumstances or about things in politics or society over which I have little control. Instead, let me be a strong Christian witness and work to change things for the better. In Jesus' name, amen.

---

59 J. Jacob Jenkins, *Buried Alive* (Baltimore: PublishAmerica, 2006), 63-66. Paraphrased.
60 Jenkins, 66.
61 Anna Shephard, *Jesus Loves You,* September 12, 2004; I heard this quoted by a member of our church in a children's message; originally attributed to St. Francis of Assisi.

42. BEING "BUSY" IS NOT THE ANSWER[62]

Ecclesiastes 2:20-21. *So I turned and gave my heart up to despair concerning all the toil of my labors under the sun, because sometimes one who has toiled with wisdom and knowledge and skill must leave all to be enjoyed by another who did not toil for it. This also is vanity and a great evil.*

Is your life so "busy" that you don't leave time for the important things? Before I retired, I led a very busy life as a corporate executive in a large manufacturing plant. My life was filled with "important" things, mostly meetings to deal with one manufacturing problem or another. My life was not my own. I was consumed with putting out "brush fires" and running from one meeting to the next; often bringing my mail and other work home to read because I ran out of time during the day. It was my wife who finally pointed out the obvious. I was going to regret not spending time with my young children when I looked back years from now and realized that they were grown, and I couldn't turn the clock back. It was a sobering moment. I won't say that it completely cured my workaholic ways. But. I brought less work home. I enjoyed my kids more. I rebalanced my life and reconsidered my priorities.

It is so easy to get caught up in being busy that we lose our perspective. In fact, I've heard many people "brag" about being too busy, like it's some kind of status symbol. We don't necessarily choose busyness; it just catches up to us and consumes us. And then, we lose direction. We tell ourselves that later in life, when we are not so busy, or when we get through this difficult time, we will get around to the important stuff like spending more time with our family and our God, taking time out to have some fun and doing some of the things on our "bucket list." So slow down! Start your day off with a devotional (like this one) and some quiet meditation time and prayer. Eat three square meals a day; not on the run but sitting down with people and enjoying the meal and the conversation. This is especially true of the evening meal with your family, where you can all "catch up" on the events of the day. Have a long-range goal in mind for your life that you work at little by little each day. Plot your course. Don't bite off more than you can chew; put

---

62   J. Jacob Jenkins, *Buried Alive* (Baltimore: PublishAmerica, 2006). 80-81. Portions paraphrased.

some downtime in your day. Rest on the Sabbath. By being intentional about your life rather than just being "busy"; you will feel much more fulfilled at the end of the day.

PRAYER: Dear Lord, Help me to not be so busy that I lose track of what is important in life. How I spend my time reveals what is important to me. I want to spend time communing with You, and loving my family and my neighbors, and using my God-given talents in a way that is pleasing to You. Help me to live a purpose-filled life that brings glory to You. In Jesus' name, amen.

43. ETERNITY STARTS NOW[63]

Hebrews 6:12. *So that you may not become sluggish, but imitators of those who through faith and patience inherit the promises.*

Are you a person of action or procrastination? Even our prayers can be a delay tactic if we're not careful about it. We are faced with a decision that calls for action, and we say, "I'll pray about it"—and then the opportunity passes us by. That's not to say that prayer isn't important; we just need to be careful not to use it as an excuse for inaction. The unattractive word for inaction is "laziness." We take life for granted. We just "drift along" aimlessly. We don't appreciate that each day is a gift of God (and may be our last). We believe that life here on earth is just a preamble for the "real" life we will share in eternity with God. Wake up! Kingdom life doesn't start when we die; it starts here and now! The things we accomplish in this life will be recognized and built upon in the next. Jesus said that "He is God not of the dead, but of the living" (Matthew 22:32). Eternity starts now. What are you waiting for? Set aside your difficult time and lay out a plan; set some short and long-term goals for yourself. "Dream as if you'll live forever. Live as if you'll die today."[64] And don't forget the all-important role of cultivating relationships—they last forever. Remember God's command to love the Lord your God with all your heart, all your soul and all your mind, and to love your neighbor as yourself (Matthew 22:38-39). Equipped with a loving attitude towards others and an action plan in your back pocket, you'll go far in this life and be prepared for the next.

PRAYER: Dear Lord, Help me to be a person of action—a person who values and cherishes each day as a gift from You and refuses to squander it. Cultivate in me a loving attitude toward my fellow Christians and help me to see clearly what actions I should be taking in this life which are pleasing to You. In Jesus' name, amen.

---

63   J. Jacob Jenkins, *Buried Alive* (Baltimore: PublishAmerica, 2006), 120-123; Portions paraphrased.
64   Jenkins, 125; Quoting James Dean.

44. THE WILES OF THE DEVIL[65]

Ephesians 6:11 (KJV). Put on the whole armor of God, that ye may be able to stand against the wiles of the devil.

We can pretty much tell when we have sin in our lives. We have the guidance of the Ten Commandments, (Exodus 20:12-17) and the "seven deadly sins" (Matthew 15:19). And, we know how to deal with the sin in our lives: we confess them to God and repent—change our ways and try not to repeat the same mistakes. But, evil that affects our lives is a much more subtle thing to detect and deal with, particularly when we are going through a difficult time. We must be wary of the "wiles of the devil" (Ephesians 6:11). "We need deliverance from the evil that doesn't look like evil, and that we are not likely to recognize as evil; evil that, in fact, looks like good."[66] The evil is hidden in the way itself. The end result may be fine—good, even—but the manner in which it is achieved is evil. Or, we may get someone to do something that in the end is beneficial, but the way that we got them to do it was deceptive or manipulative or de-personalizing. Evil is especially prone to exist in large institutions, according to the studies and work of Jacques Ellul, a French sociologist. "The basic good of money is idolized into the god of Mammon, the basic good of language is debased into the lies of propaganda, the basic good of technology is depersonalized into a world of non-relationship."[67] I spent forty years of my life working for a large corporation, and, while there were many positive experiences from this work, and I now have a comfortable retirement, I saw many instances of the subtle forces of evil within the organization. Our performance was boiled down to one "competency rating," which was the basis of our pay raise—a very impersonal, and sometimes politically motivated way of evaluating a person's contribution to the organization. A person's status was often based on where he was placed on the organization chart and his association with the "in" crowd rather than his true abilities. One need look no further than Wall Street to see evil in the form of greed permeating

---

65 Eugene H. Peterson, *Practice Resurrection: A Conversation on Growing Up in Christ* (Grand Rapids, Wm. B. Eerdmans, 2010), Kindle, 2950-2980; Portions paraphrased.
66 Peterson, 2957.
67 Peterson, 2979.

the institution. So be on the lookout for subtle forms of evil. How do we combat it? By putting on the "full armor of God": truth, righteousness, peace, faith, salvation, and the Word of God (Ephesians 6:13-17). We don't combat it through violence; we combat it by being Christians: *we* are the weapons against the devil's wiles. Who we are takes precedence over what we do. Stand firm in the faith; stand firm and take on God's blessings; stand firm in the church; stand firm in the Spirit. You will prevail.

PRAYER: Dear Lord, Help me to recognize evil masquerading as goodness. Help me to stand firm in the faith against the devil's wiles by putting on the full armor of God. As a Christian, I know that You have provided me with all the tools to combat the evil in this world. In Jesus' name, amen.

45. THE RIVER OF LIFE

Revelation 22:1-2a. *Then the angel showed me the river of the water of life, bright as crystal, flowing from the throne of God and of the Lamb, through the middle of the street of the city.*

I am contemplative at heart. I described the method of centering prayer earlier (see Reflection 20), and I commit 20 minutes twice a day every day to this method. There is a wonderful book by Richard Rohr entitled *Everything Belongs* that describes the benefits of contemplative prayer. The chapter that spoke to me is titled, "The Spirit as a River" where Rohr compares the love of God through the Holy Spirit as a river that flows through us.[68] He says that when we concentrate on just us—our story, our difficult times and tribulations—we miss the Great Person that we are. The Spirit is described as "living water" and "a spring of water gushing up to eternal life" (John 4:10-14), and in Revelation as a "river . . . of life" (Revelation 22:1-2). Rohr believes "that faith might be precisely that ability to trust the river, to trust the flow and the river. It is a process that we don't have to change, coerce or improve. We need to allow it to flow." This requires an effort to get out of our head knowledge and into the recognition that we are a part of something that is greater than us: God's love. At times, we need to give up our goal-orientation and our focus on the particulars and get to the point where we aren't "pushing the river" but are content to be awash in it. I hope that this metaphor of the river speaks to you as strongly as it does to me. There is a comfort in realizing that we are part of something greater than us—a river of love.

PRAYER: Dear Lord, Thank You for the metaphor of the river of life flowing through and around me. I'm beginning to realize that there is more to life than just me and my pre-conceived notions of what life is about. We are all connected in a "river of life" and I am comforted by being awash in Your love. In Jesus' name, amen.

---

68 Richard Rohr, *Everything Belongs: The Gift of Contemplative Prayer* (New York: Crossroad, 2003), 142-143.

46. BEING EMBRACED BY THE LORD

Song of Solomon 2:6. *O that his left hand were under my head, and that his right hand embraced me.*

If your difficult time is one of physical suffering or psychological turmoil due to seeing a loved one suffer, I have found this metaphor from Thomas Keating to be of great help. According to Keating's understanding of the fathers of the Church, God embraces us with both arms (see the verse above from Song of Solomon).

"With the left, He humbles and corrects us; with the right He lifts us up and consoles us with the assurance of being loved by him. If you want to be fully embraced by the Lord, you have to accept both arms: the one that allows suffering for the sake of purification and the one that brings the joy of union. When you feel physical pain or when psychological struggles are persecuting you, you should think that God is hugging you extra tightly. Trials are an expression of His Love, not of rejection."[69]

It is so hard to be comforted when you are in pain, but perhaps by thinking of it as Keating's being "hugged extra tightly" by God, you can endure it and even grow in grace by it.

PRAYER: Dear Lord, Help me to endure my physical pain by considering it an extra tight hug by You. I don't pretend to understand why we must suffer, but Christ did, and so must we in our journey here on earth. Help us to understand what You are trying to teach us through our suffering and give us the perspective to know that "this too shall pass." In Jesus' name, amen.

---

69 Thomas Keating, *The Daily Reader for Contemplative Living: Excerpts from the Works of Father Thomas Keating* (New York: Continuum, 2006), 12.

47. BEING OBEDIENT

John 14:21. *They who have my commandments and keep them are those who love me; and those who love me will be loved by my Father, and I will love them and reveal myself to them.*

Let's see what Eugene Peterson says about the tricky topic of obedience. Now that Christ has died for our sins, and we are living under His grace, we can do whatever we want, right? Not exactly. Dietrich Bonhoeffer calls this thinking "cheap grace," and the apostle Paul makes it clear that obedience to God's ways is still a precious thing (see Romans 6:1-2). But, neither is obedience a task of drudgery and gloom. The faithful Christian obeys out of his love for Jesus and His ways, and he practices the "fruit of the Spirit": "love, joy, peace, patience, kindness, generosity, faithfulness, gentleness, and self-control. There is no law against such things" (Galatians 5:22-23). Plus, obedience isn't just looking back and feeling guilty about our shortcomings or being obsessed with our difficult time. It has a future element to it—a hopeful element. Eugene Peterson says, "If we define the nature of our lives by the mistake of the moment or the defeat of the hour or the burden of the day, we will define it wrongly. We need roots in the past to give obedience ballast and breadth; we need a vision of the future to give obedience direction and a goal."[70] He points out that we need to have a perspective that is bigger than the scope of our own lives or a snapshot in time: our God is bigger and greater than our own limited perspective! And, it is when we can see our lives in the context of the grander landscape of God's Kingdom, that obedience makes sense. "For Christian faith cannot be comprehended by examining an instamatic flash picture which has caught a pose of beauty or absurdity, ecstasy or terror; it is a full revelation of a vast creation and a grandly consummated redemption."[71] Obedience, when seen in this context is not so much of a chore. It is instead having "an accurate memory of God's ways, combined with a lively hope in his promises."[72] We learn God's ways from the Bible, and we can find out how things turn out for people who go their own way and think they know better

---

70 Eugene H. Peterson, *A Long Obedience in the Same Direction: Discipleship in an Instant Society* (Downers Grove: InterVarsity Press, 1980), 165.
71 Peterson, 166.
72 Peterson, 166.

than God. So, the memory part is readily available and time-tested. Want to try it differently and disobey? You are flaunting all the wisdom of the Bible. And, the hopeful part of obedience is marveling at God's great provision for our lives and partaking of it—thankfully and obediently.

PRAYER: Dear Lord, Thank You for all the stories in the Bible which keep me grounded and aware of the path of obedience. And thank You for the hope that I have in the future, brought about by an awareness of the magnificence of Your Kingdom and my obedient response to Your love. In Jesus' name, amen.

48. LEAP OF FAITH

Matthew 14:30. *"But when [Peter] noticed the strong wind, he became frightened, and beginning to sink, he cried out, "Lord, save me!"*

When it comes to embracing our faith and minimizing doubt that invariably comes with our difficult time, we must remember these words from John Ortberg, "Once we have been born, trying to put off deciding what to do about God is like jumping off a diving board and trying to put off actually entering the water."[73] He has another good analogy about jumping and faith. Let's say that you're on the fifth floor of a burning building: the elevator doesn't work; the stairs are aflame, and there is no escape except for jumping out the window into a blanket that several firemen are holding. The blanket appears thin; the firemen look a little unsteady, but you most likely will jump. Why? Because it is the best shot at achieving your purpose, survival. You are not in the probability calculating game—you are in survival mode. Faith is like that: it's your best shot at survival—for eternity. We can't possibly know whether all of God's promises are true without faith, including the ultimate promise that when we die, we'll have eternal life. But, we do have God's word and the Holy Spirit to help us in our faith journey and other Christians to pray for us and help us in periods of doubt. So, the "leap of faith" looks like our best alternative. It's certainly the one that God is behind.

PRAYER: Dear Lord, In my difficult time, help me to make the "leap of faith" and trust in Your provisions for my life. I know that from time to time I will have my doubts, but You are with me in all phases of my life. Thank You for the gift of the Holy Spirit and my church and other Christians to help me through the difficult times and restore my perspective that You love me and have a plan for me. In Jesus' name, amen.

---

73   John Ortberg, *Faith and Doubt* (Grand Rapids: Zondervan, 2008), 30.

49. SACRED WOUNDS[74]

Job 34:6. In spite of being right I am counted a liar; my wound is incurable, though I am without transgression.

An unwounded, "innocent" Christian who has not learned life's lessons yet through suffering is not able to live a full life. Consider this hypothetical man: He is the one who appears to have his act together: white, middle class, healthy, "sinless," "happy," drives a classy car, wears the latest clothing styles. The man is holding things together although inside things are tending to fall apart and spin out of control. Of course, things are not all bad, but, at some point, he needs to acknowledge the darker aspects of life such as his feeling that there is "something more"; feelings of despair and perhaps even jealousy of others who appear to have their act more together than he does. He needs to allow himself to be wounded. There is something about a humiliating wound, a wound that is quite undeserved, that becomes something sacred and instructive. The wound is undeserved in the sense that you did nothing specific to "earn" it other than living in your own sin nature. What you are going through just doesn't seem "fair." "Allowing our always-unjust wounds to, in fact, become sacred wounds, is the unique Christian name for salvation. One always learns one's mystery at the price of one's innocence."[75] In other words, you don't grow if you don't acknowledge life's difficulties and let them "wound" you. There is something "larger than life" that happens when you abandon yourself to hurts that are beyond your control to "fix." You turn them over to God. You recognize that they are out of your control. You grow. So, your difficult circumstances may be your path to salvation! Let God speak to you through them and embrace the mystery.

PRAYER: Dear Lord, I never thought of my difficult time as a necessary component to my faith journey. I'd rather have my act together than suffer and be wounded. But, I must abandon myself to my difficulties, and let my wound show me the path to salvation. Help me to accept the things that are out of my control and through them, grow. In Jesus' name, amen.

---

74 Richard Rohr, *Hope Against Darkness: The Transforming Vision of Saint Francis in an Age of Anxiety* (Cincinnati: St. Anthony Messenger Press, 2001), Kindle, 1085-1090; Portions paraphrased.

75 Rohr, 1089.

50. THE SKEPTIC, THE CYNIC, AND THE REBEL

John 20:25b. Unless I see the mark of the nails in his hands and put my finger in the mark of the nails and put my hand in his side, I will not believe.

There are many people who are filled with doubts about their faith. John Ortberg characterizes three main types of doubters: the skeptic, the cynic, and the rebel.[76] The skeptic is one who suspends judgment and does not commit himself because the demand for sufficient evidence has not yet been met. The disciple Thomas is a good example of a skeptic. He was not present when the disciples first saw the resurrected Jesus, and, when they told him about it, he said, "Unless I see the mark of the nails in his hands and put my finger in the mark of the nails and put my hand in his side, I will not believe" (John 20:25). Jesus later satisfied this request, and said, "Have you believed because you have seen me? Blessed are those who have not seen and yet have come to believe" (John 20:29). We are among that group who has not seen yet believe, and we have Christ's blessing. Next, the cynic offers conclusions about the world that paint it in an entirely negative light. They not only point out what is wrong with the world but also lack the courage to do something about it—they are afraid to accept responsibility. Pontius Pilate, the Roman curator who tried Jesus, is an example. He cynically asks, "What is Truth?" (John 18:38). What he really meant was, "How can you truly be certain of anything? What difference does it make?" He was not so much seeking answers as trying to avoid responsibility for crucifying Jesus. He ultimately "washed his hands" of the whole ordeal. Finally, the rebel exhibits the severest form of doubt. He not only doesn't believe, but he also doesn't *want* to believe, and he wants to convince you why. Saul, during his persecution days before he became an apostle, was a rebel. He was intent on obliterating the Christians from off the face of the earth. Fortunately, he had his Damascus road experience, and became as fervent a Christian as he was an opponent. All these examples of doubters have been explained to show that there is a real opposition to faithful people. We may not be able to convert them, but we must understand where they are coming from to relate to them and treat them as worthwhile people who are

---

76   John Ortberg, *Faith and Doubt* (Grand Rapids: Zondervan, 2008), 123-132.

going through a difficult time due to upbringing or circumstances. My prayer is that you make it through your difficult time without becoming skeptical or cynical or rebellious. It takes a great deal of humility and soul-searching to overcome your doubts and stay the course.

PRAYER: Dear Lord, Help me not to be skeptical, cynical, or rebellious during my difficult time. Also, help me to identify these tendencies in other people and to love them unconditionally. Life is a struggle sometimes, and we need to understand one another and to develop a personal relationship with You to make it through the day. In Jesus' name, amen.

51. GOD VS. POSSESSIONS[77]

Matthew 19:21. Jesus said to him, "If you wish to be perfect, go, sell your possessions, and give the money to the poor, and you will have treasure in heaven; then come, follow me."

Perhaps your difficult time centers around being too attached to your possessions. Kingdom living involves continuous growth and a "letting go" of possessions. We can't ever get too comfortable with our understanding of God's ways—there is always more to learn, and that is a good thing. As Anthony Bloom puts it, "we must rejoice that poor as we are, we are so rich; yet, we must long for the true riches of the Kingdom, being careful not to be beguiled by what we already possess so that we turn away from what is ahead of us."[78] And, that leads us to possessions—they get in the way of Kingdom living. When you latch on to a possession, say it's something you can grasp in your hand like a watch, then you can't do anything else with your hand. So, it is with your heart: if you set your heart on your riches, you close it in and cut it off from reaching out to embrace God's love. Your heart becomes as small as the thing that you set your heart on. We cannot go Godward until our hands and heart are freed of preoccupation with possessions. Then our prayer life takes off and we appreciate that all we have is a gift from God. Certainly, we are to enjoy our possessions—God gave them to us. However, we can't be preoccupied with them.

PRAYER: Thank You, Lord, for my possessions. They are a gift from You for my enjoyment. Just don't let me get so attached to them that they take precedence over my love for You. I know that hands full of "stuff" are not free to do Your Kingdom work, and the same goes for my heart. Getting to know You is a continuous growth process. Help my endeavors to "love the Lord [my] God with all [my] heart, and with all [my] soul, and with all [my] mind" (Matthew 22:37). In Jesus' name, amen.

---

77 Anthony Bloom, *Beginning to Pray* (New York: Paulist Press, 1970), 38-40; Portions paraphrased.
78 Bloom, 40.

52. DELVING INTO SCRIPTURE[79]

2 Timothy 3:16. *All scripture is inspired by God and is useful for teaching, for reproof, for correction, and for training in righteousness.*

Are you having trouble trudging your way through the Bible? Perhaps you have given it up entirely in your difficult time. Some of Scripture seems so mundane, down in the trenches, dealing with people you'd rather not know. That is part of the beauty of the Bible. God works through real people. People with problems and flaws just like you and I have. The Bible is not reserved for the pious and pure. The Bible is not full of abstract ideas that we need to philosophize about. The Bible shows people struggling in their "here and now" so that we can see parallels in our own lives. The result is quite amazing. As Richard Rohr says, "The marvelous anthology of books and letters called the Bible is all for the sake of astonishment! It's for divine transformation, not intellectual or "small-self" coziness."[80] The intent is not to throw a bunch of ideas at us to see if we "get it." The intent is to give us a new set of eyes to see things with the help of the Holy Spirit that we didn't see before. Rohr implores us to read the Bible with a "beginner's mind"—setting aside our prejudices, our "know it all" attitude, our pseudo-certainty and smugness about life, and beholding things afresh. One of the pre-conceived notions that many people bring with them as they read the Bible is that God is to be feared: He is judgmental; He expects us to "toe the line," and He wreaks havoc if we do not. God's love is to be earned, and we resent it. Rohr says, "The only way [for our perspective to change] is to change the power equation and invite us into a world of mutuality and vulnerability. Our living image of that power change is called Jesus!"[81] Jesus, who is fully God and fully human, is "gentle and humble" in nature, and He shows us how to relate to God by understanding the true nature of God: He is merciful, gracious, faithful, forgiving, and steadfast in love. It is up to us to experience that as we read the text. Rohr points out that it requires openness, vulnerability, and a willingness to "go inside" instead of staying at the surface. He implores us to be willing to take

---

79 Richard Rohr, *Things Hidden: Scripture as Spirituality* (Cincinnati: St. Anthony Messenger Press), Kindle, 170-208; Portions paraphrased.
80 Rohr, 170.
81 Rohr, 208.

the three steps forward and two steps backward that often appear in the text. The Bible is "text in travail," which mirrors what we are going through. "The Bible offers both mature and immature responses to almost everything, and you have to learn the difference."[82] Hopefully, these words have re-kindled in you a desire to delve into Scripture despite your difficult time and "point you toward an inner awareness of the Spirit that is guiding you right now."[83]

PRAYER: Dear Lord, I am going to try to read Scripture with a new set of eyes and enter this "text in travail" so that I might draw parallels to my own circumstances and, through them, grow. Help me to overcome my prejudices and false assumptions about who God is, and, instead, learn with a "beginner's mind" about His true nature and unconditional love for me. In Jesus' name, amen.

---

82 Richard Rohr, *Things Hidden: Scripture as Spirituality* (Cincinnati: St. Anthony Messenger Press), 262.
83 Rohr, 281.

53. GOD COMING TO US DISGUISED AS OUR LIFE

Matthew 4:18b-19. [Peter and Andrew were] casting a net into the sea— for they were fishermen. And he said to them, "Follow me, and I will make you fish for people."

Many people try to separate the spiritual from their everyday world. The Bible states otherwise: "The Biblical revelation is saying that we are already spiritual beings; we just don't know it yet. The Bible tries to let you in on the secret, by revealing God in the ordinary. That's why so much of the text seems so mundane, practical, specific and frankly, unspiritual!"[84] God lives "down in the trenches" with us in our everyday "grind it out," "dog eat dog," filled with difficulties world. It is comforting that He does so. Richard Rohr says that "it is our experiences that transform us if we are willing to experience our experiences all the way through."[85] To "experience things all the way through" means to experience things deeply, as though they meant everything to us; the experience is all-consuming to us. When we go through suffering and trials, it is often during these times that we are drawn closest to God and experience transformation. The Bible provides plenty of examples. We hear stories of sin and war, adulteries and affairs, kings and killings, intrigues and deceits—the ordinary, wonderful, and sad events of human life. Rohr says that it is "God coming to us disguised as our life."[86] It is all about personal relationships and working through them, including that most personal of all—our relationship with God. So, turn to your Bible in your difficult time, and see your life mirrored in the stories it tells. God is with you in your day-to-day struggles.

PRAYER: Dear Lord, Sometimes it hard to "stay the course." But I can learn from similar stories to mine in the Bible that You are especially present in the "here and now," and that You work best with us in our normal daily activities, not in some rare, theoretical spiritual "fix." Help me to "experience my experiences all the way through" so that I am transformed into Your likeness. In Jesus' name, amen.

---

84 Richard Rohr, *Things Hidden: Scripture as Spirituality* (Cincinnati: St. Anthony Messenger Press), 330.
85 Rohr, 320.
86 Rohr, 330.

54. LIVING "BETWEEN THE TIMES"

Ephesians 6:11. *Put on the whole armor of God, so that you may be able to stand against the wiles of the devil.*

We live "between the times" as Shirley Guthrie would characterize it.[87] A time when the Kingdom is here but not fulfilled yet until Christ's return. That means there is still evil to deal with, as you well know in your difficult time. At times, the world situation seems bleak, almost irrevocably so. Political battles surround us, wars and threats of war exist, even in our churches there is sometimes political infighting and backstabbing going on that seems so far out of place. So, what do we do? Just wring our hands and give up? Not so, says Guthrie. "Christians cannot be ultimately pessimistic and gloomy about the world, the church and themselves. No matter how hopeless the situation may seem, they know of a power at work here and now greater than the power of evil, a power that keeps breaking into our godless and godforsaken world to heal old wounds, make new beginnings, and (if only now and then, here and there) give us a glimpse of the final victory of God's compassion and justice that are on the way."[88] I hope that even in your difficult time, you catch those glimpses of God's compassion and justice and do not give up. There is still so much good on this earth, even though our newscasts portray a world in disarray. Make no mistake; evil is still here and must be combatted. "But if we believe that since Easter the powers of evil are fighting a losing battle, and that the one who has already conquered them is still at work to finish what he began, then we can take heart, nevertheless to keep fighting however powerful the enemy without and within may seem."[89]

PRAYER: Dear Lord, I am so thankful that evil is fighting a losing battle, even during my difficult time. Help me to put on the full armor of God and to resist the devil's ways. True, things may look bleak now, but Christ has won the ultimate victory, which will come to full fruition when He returns, and, in the meantime, I can fight the good fight. In Jesus' name, amen.

---

87 Shirley C. Guthrie, *Christian Doctrine* (Louisville: Westminster John Knox, 1994), 286.
88 Guthrie, 285.
89 Guthrie, 286.

55. ABOUT FAITH

Exodus 3:2. There the angel of the LORD appeared to [Moses] in a flame of fire out of a bush; he looked and the bush was blazing, yet it was not consumed.

Most people that I know want to be certain in their faith. They want to have God all figured out and in their pocket so that they can call upon Him when they need Him and are pretty sure how He will respond, or, at least, how they will request Him to respond. But Richard Rohr asserts just the opposite, "The very concept of faith [is] the freedom not to know because I am known more fully than I know or even need to know."[90] We can't possibly know everything there is to know about God, and that's OK. We can relax in our faith because He knows us better, and that is sufficient! Of course, we should endeavor to learn all that we can about God, through reading the Bible, attending Sunday School and small groups, and participating in worship. This is especially important as you go through your difficult time. We want the comfort and peace that comes with knowing our Beloved. But just like there is mystery and an unknown aspect to those we love the most, so it is with God. Cherish the part you do not understand. It makes God greater than you, where He belongs.

PRAYER: Dear Lord, I long to know You completely, but I realize that is not possible. Help me to be content in knowing that You know me more fully than I know or even need to know You. There is a mystery about You that is comforting when I let it be. You are full of surprises for my life and that is a good thing. How bland life would be if I had You all figured out! Be with me through my difficult time and give me hope that You have untold riches in store for me! In Jesus' name, amen.

---

90 Richard Rohr, *Things Hidden: Scripture as Spirituality* (Cincinnati: St. Anthony Messenger Press), 373.

56. DESIRE[91]

Mark 10:51a. *"What do you want me to do for you?"*

Most people regard having desires for things as not good when thinking religiously. And, that holds true for material and self-serving wishes like a new car or house or financial gain. But, consider that without any desire, there would be no sense in getting up in the morning—you wouldn't feel like doing anything. Desire is what drives us to change, to excel, to feel strongly, to achieve. And, when it comes to God, desire is what makes us seek Him. Recognizing our desires means recognizing God's desires for us. Jesus could have just healed the blind man, Bartimaeus, outright—He knew that Bartimaeus was blind. But, He asked the man, "What do you want me to do for you?" (Mark 10:46-52). He did it not so much for Himself, but for the blind man. "Jesus was helping the man identify his desire, and to be clear about it."[92] It helps us articulate what we want from God and clarifies our position with Him. It is freeing to say, "This is what I desire in life." When we tell God our desires, our relationship with Him deepens—God leads us to discover who we are and what we are meant to do, even to the point of helping to determine our vocation, or how to get out of our difficult circumstances. So, it doesn't hurt to pray for our desires, if they are sincere and well-intentioned and focused on helping us better understand God's plan for our lives.

PRAYER: Dear Lord, I have lots of desires in life. Help me to express those desires to You in ways that improve our relationship and make me understand Your plan for my life better. In Jesus' name, amen.

---

91 James Martin, SJ, *The Jesuit Guide to (Almost) Everything: A Spirituality for Real Life* (New York: HarperCollins, 2010), 57-58; Portions paraphrased.
92 Martin, SJ, 58.

57. THE SACRED WOUND[93]

2 Corinthians 1:6-7. If we are being afflicted, it is for your consolation and salvation; if we are being consoled, it is for your consolation, which you experience when you patiently endure the same sufferings that we are also suffering. Our hope for you is unshaken; for we know that as you share in our sufferings, so also you share in our consolation.

Richard Rohr defines suffering as "whenever you are not in control."[94] Your life has been taken over by a condition that eludes your personal ability to cope. You must turn over your suffering to the care and nurture of others and to the mercy of God. You must become vulnerable and approachable. You must be willing to go down before you can find your way up again. When seen in the context of the Big Picture (see Reflection 37), suffering takes on cosmic and personal significance: the great historical figures of the Bible suffered, especially Christ Himself—it is part of our journey. Rohr says that we must find a way to realize that God is somehow intimately involved in our suffering and uses it as part of His transforming plan for our lives. Otherwise, we run the risk of becoming bitter and not knowing where to pile up the burden of our own sinfulness and brokenness. Try to see your suffering and your difficult time from God's perspective, knowing that God upholds you in all circumstances, and that He will never forsake you or abandon you.

PRAYER: Dear Lord, Help me to sense Your presence when I suffer. Help me to see the Big Picture of Your love for me despite my difficult circumstances. I know that suffering breaks down my arrogance and my tendency to think too highly of myself. With patience, I await the day when I will suffer no longer. In Jesus' name, amen.

---

93 Richard Rohr, *Things Hidden: Scripture as Spirituality* (Cincinnati: St. Anthony Messenger Press), 447-449; Portions paraphrased.
94 Rohr, 447.

58. MADE IN GOD'S IMAGE[95]

Genesis 1:27a. *So God created humankind in his image, in the image of God he created them.*

Many of us can't get out of our sin/total depravity mindset to realize that we are first and foremost children of God and created in His image. We are spiritual beings and are united with God and carry about His likeness within us. So, before we get down on ourselves during our difficult time or think that we aren't worthy of God's love, let's marvel at our belongingness. "It's not that *if* I am moral, *then* I will be loved by God, but rather I must first come to experience God's love, and then I will—almost naturally, be moral."[96] We think that we are far too important in the equation when it comes to deserving God's love—our ego gets in the way. And yet, we tell ourselves, "I am not worthy," even though the Bible points out time and time again that worthiness is not the question, through countless stories of people who, in their own right, are not worthy. Being in relationship with a loving God is the question; a God who has declared everything He created, including us, to be "very good" (Genesis 1:31). That should be very comforting to you in your difficult time. We needn't be so obsessed with getting right with God. We are made in His image! "It is not a 'those who do it right get to go to heaven' thing, as much as it is a 'those who live like me are in heaven now' thing!"[97]

PRAYER: Dear Lord, Thank You for creating me in Your image and declaring me and Your entire creation "very good." It is comforting to reflect on the fact that I am a spiritual being who enjoys a special relationship with You. Let me mirror Your goodness in my day-to-day activities so that I can experience the Kingdom of God here and now. In Jesus' name, amen.

---

95 Richard Rohr, *Things Hidden: Scripture as Spirituality* (Cincinnati: St. Anthony Messenger Press), 520-522; Portions paraphrased.
96 Rohr, 522.
97 Rohr, 608.

59. FLOURISHING VS. LANGUISHING

Psalm 72:7. *In his days, may righteousness flourish and peace abound, until the moon is no more.*

Even during your difficult time, you can be either flourishing or languishing. John Ortberg provides some tips for you to distinguish between the two.[98] If you are flourishing, you have a zest for life, and you realize that life is much more than the external "power" symbols of status, prestige, and money. In fact, it's not primarily about you at all but about the strength of your relationships, especially to God. You see your life as God's project, and you know that God is more concerned with you reaching your full potential than you are. You are comfortable with whom God made you to be, and you don't wish that you were someone else. You have a sense of expectancy about the upcoming day. Things matter—each moment is a God-filled gift. If you are languishing, you feel uneasy and discontent inside. You are drawn to bad habits: too much TV, too much alcohol, misusing sex, and excess spending. Your thoughts drift toward fear or anger. You think about yourself a good deal and not in a good way. Relationally, you are troubled and resort to sarcasm, gossip, and flattery. You isolate. You dominate. You attack. You withdraw. I hope that you are flourishing, or that you can see in these reflections the attributes that are desirable and begin the process of change. With God's help, that will enable you to live a flourishing life. God wants that for you.

PRAYER: Dear Lord, Thank You for these examples of a flourishing life. I must admit that due to my difficult circumstances, I let myself slip into self-pity, and I don't seek the best path—I slip into languishing. Help me to see Your Hand in my life and to realize that You want the best for me and that You have a plan for me. Give me patience and a bigger perspective of life and love that draws me out of my languishing and moves me toward flourishing. In Jesus' name, amen.

---

98 John Ortberg, *The Me I Want To Be: The Me I Want to Be: Becoming God's Best Version of You* (Grand Rapids: Zondervan, 2009), 11-21.

60. THE ME I WANT TO BE

Ephesians 4:22-24. *You were taught to put away your former way of life, your old self, corrupt and deluded by its lusts, and to be renewed in the spirit of your minds, and to clothe yourselves with the new self, created according to the likeness of God in true righteousness and holiness.*

As an aid to understanding yourself during this time of difficulty, John Ortberg discusses several obstacles to being your true self.[99] First, there is "the me I *pretend* to be." We try to convince people of our worth, while secretly feeling unworthy. A lot of people put on a façade, for example, naming other important people that they associate with or spectacular places they have visited, as though that gives them respect and credibility. Then, there is "the me I think I *should* be" which may very well be at odds with the person God wants you to be. You will come to know the parts of you that are inconsistent with the person God wants you to be—let those parts die. "It will be a death of the lesser self, a false self, so that a better and nobler self can come to life."[100] Next, comes "the me other people want me to be": some people would like to use you to further their own interests. You may have to disappoint them to stay true to yourself. That's a part of the give and take of love—you just can't please everyone all the time. After that comes "the me I'm afraid God wants," which usually means that you try too hard to follow all the rules as though God's love is conditional upon your perfection. "Jesus did not say, 'I have come that you might follow the rules.' He said, 'I have come that you might have life, and have it with abundance.'" Then there is "the me that fails to be," or as Ortberg calls it "failure to thrive."[101] It is characterized by a weariness of soul and an inability to delight in life. Instead, embrace "the me I am meant to be," which is to grow and flourish and become the person God designed you to be. It doesn't come overnight; it takes a lot of prayer and courage and discernment, but it is our life's chief endeavor.

99   John Ortberg, *The Me I Want To Be: The Me I Want to Be: Becoming God's Best Version of You* (Grand Rapids: Zondervan, 2009), 22-32.
100 Ortberg, 26.
101 Ortberg, 28-30.

PRAYER: Dear Lord, As I struggle through my difficult time, help me to find "the me I am meant to be." I know it won't be easy or instantaneous, but, with patience and prayer and the help of my fellow Christians, I can grow in the way that is pleasing to You. The other ways of living that are described in this reflection are superficial and do not stand the test of time. I pray for discernment as I embark on this path of service and love. In Jesus' name, amen.

61. THE RESURRECTED LIFE

Revelation 21:2. And I saw the holy city, the new Jerusalem, coming down out of heaven from God, prepared as a bride adorned for her husband.

People who are suffering through a difficult time will benefit from the following reflection about life after death. There is a lot of confusion about what happens when we die and what happens when Christ returns. The person who has set things right with me is N.T. Wright, a prolific writer, historian, and Bishop of Durham for the Church of England. In his wonderful book *Surprised by Hope*, Dr. Wright presents the resurrected life in Biblically accurate terms. Here are his points about the resurrection. First, when we die, we will be in Paradise. Christ said to the thief on the cross next to Him, "Truly I tell you, today you will be with me in Paradise" (Luke 23:43). We will not go into an unconscious state of nothingness while we wait for Christ's return. Otherwise, why would the apostle Paul have said, "I am hard pressed between the two: my desire is to depart and be with Christ, for that is far better; but to remain in the flesh is more necessary for you" (Philippians 1:23-24). He would not have been anxious to depart into a world of nothingness. The Bible says very little about Paradise, but it probably most resembles what most Christians think of as "heaven"—a place of pure bliss and happiness and contentment in a garden-like setting. Then, there is the all-important time of Christ's second coming, where we are all resurrected in bodily form to reside in the New Jerusalem, which "[comes] down out of heaven from God" (Revelation 21:2). This is where most Christians get it wrong. We don't "go up to heaven when we die"; instead heaven is revealed to us here on earth. This has profound significance for how we live our lives here and now. What we do now has relevance for God's Kingdom and will be built upon when Christ returns. Rather than think of some future existence "up in heaven," it is better to think of doing things now "on earth as it is in heaven" (the Lord's Prayer, Matthew 6:9-13). As Wright says, "Heaven, in the Bible, is not a future destiny but the other, hidden dimension of our ordinary life—God's dimension, if you like. God made heaven and earth; at the last he will remake both and join them together forever."[102] Read Revelation 21 and 22 in this light. It is a tremendous source of hope not just for our future existence but for our present circumstances. We are truly people of hope, and the church is a place where people gather together to share hope and be people of hope in this world. Despite your difficult circumstances, you can hold onto this source of hope.

PRAYER: Dear Lord, Thank You for Your promise to return and give us all renewed, resurrected bodies to carry on the work of the Kingdom. What we do now counts, and we strive to do things "on earth as it is in heaven." In light of Your promises, we are people of hope, and, while we may suffer and go through trials, they pale in significance to the glory that is ours in Christ Jesus. In Jesus' name, amen.

---

102 N.T. Wright, *Surprised by Hope: Rethinking Heaven, the Resurrection, and the Mission of the Church* (New York: HarperOne, 2008), 19.

62. YOUR PRIMARY FOCUS

Psalm 36:8b-9. *You give them drink from the river of your delights. For with you is the fountain of life: in your light we see light.*

"When your primary focus is being present with God, everything else has a way of falling into place. When your primary focus becomes anything else, your inner vitality suffers, and you become a lesser version of yourself."[103] So easy to say, so hard to do. We are so conditioned by our culture and environment to be self-sufficient, stand on our own, and do it our own way. That it is hard to let go. We think we must overcome our difficult time on our own. John Ortberg claims that the only way to fill the gap between the "me we are right now" and the "me that God intended us to be," is to rely on God's grace—NOT our own efforts. There is a "river of life" that flows through us (see Reflection 45), which is part and parcel the Holy Spirit working in our lives. Sometimes, we just need to jump in the river and go with the flow. In fact, Ortberg insists, "The only way to become the person God made you to be is to live with the Spirit of God flowing through you like a river of living water."[104] We have recently talked a lot about "flourishing" (see Reflection 59). Ortberg points out, "Any time you see life flourishing, it is receiving nourishment from beyond itself."[105] I'm sure that you have been around people that have a spark and a vitality to them, and it makes you wonder how they can be so full of life. Now you know. They are in the river. They see the Big Picture and are comfortable with their role in it. They are not trying to make it on their own or getting in God's way. You too, can flourish. Ask God to give you discernment and to help you get into the river. It's never too late.

PRAYER: Dear Lord, Please help me to learn how to embrace the river of life and to let You fill the gap between the me that I am and the me that You want me to be. It almost sounds too easy, but I let my ego and pursuit of selfish things get in the way. Thank You for the Holy Spirit who gives me glimpses into the Kingdom and is there to be called upon whenever I struggle with having it my way. In Jesus' name, amen.

---

103 John Ortberg, *The Me I Want To Be: The Me I Want to Be: Becoming God's Best Version of You* (Grand Rapids: Zondervan, 2009), 35.
104 Ortberg, 39.
105 Ortberg, 42.

63. MUSIC AS MEDICINE[106]

Psalm 150:4. *Praise him with tambourine and dance; praise him with strings and pipe!*

Music is important to me, and it can serve as a useful source of religious inspiration. We usually hear music in the background as something to accompany other things that we are doing. Instead, carve out periods where you are intentional about your music listening, what Roger Walsh calls "mindful listening."[107] Try choosing a favorite piece of music, preferably one that is gentle and soothing, or one that has spiritual significance to you. Take a moment to relax, sitting comfortably, and listen and enjoy it as fully as you can. Occasionally, your mind will drift into other thoughts, which is OK; simply return your attention gently to the music. This exercise develops concentration and greater sensitivity and clarity of awareness. You will become more aware of the subtleties in the music and phraseology that awakens something deep inside you. Once, when I was unable to sleep during my cancer treatments, I "conducted" the entire Berlioz "Symphonie Fantastique" while I was in my bed. It was an incredible experience and spoke deeply to my spirit. In your difficult time, try music as a form of restorative medicine. You will be calmer and more ready to face life's challenges as a result.

PRAYER: Dear Lord, I do love music, but I admit that I usually treat it casually as something in the background. Help me to be more attentive to how a soothing musical piece is speaking to me, so that I am more appreciative of life and have a calmer outlook about it. In Jesus' name, amen.

---

106 Roger Walsh, *Essential Spirituality: The 7 Central Practices to Awaken Heart and Mind* (New York: John Wiley and Sons, 1999), 185-186; Portions paraphrased.
107 Walsh, 186.

64. SURRENDER

Psalm 30:10. Hear, O LORD, and be gracious to me! O LORD, be my helper!

I want to be in control of my life; the day-to-day decisions, my finances, my sex life, how I relate to others, the whole ball of wax. But, God has a different idea. Surrender is the name of His game. That means putting Him in the driver's seat. Hard to do. Our ego gets in the way. Our difficult time gets in the way. The "ways of this world" get in the way. Everything in our culture says, "Be a man; take control; do it your way." But John Ortberg insists, "You receive power through the act of surrender that you cannot obtain any other way; you receive freedom through submission that you will otherwise never know."[108] Ortberg asserts that doesn't mean that we sit back and let God do all the work. He has given us creativity and initiative and a purpose in life. It means we don't need to worry so much about the *outcomes* of what we do. "I love my children the best I can, but I am not in charge of their destiny. I work the best I can, but I am not in control of the results. I try to make wise choices to save for retirement, but I am not running the stock market. *I find that every moment I worry is a chance to practice letting go of the need to control outcomes.*"[109] I am wary of people who say, "I prayed, and God opened up the parking space right in front of the store." I don't think that God works at that level of specificity. He didn't make us robots—He gave us a free will. But, I am learning to put more trust in God for the decisions I make; not that He "spoon feeds" me, but that I needn't worry that I'm all alone in my decisions. I think that God is most concerned about the *process* of life and the *relationships* of life rather than the specific results of my actions. The process is what builds my character and makes me more Christ-like.

PRAYER: Dear Lord, Thank You for being in the driver's seat and taking on life's worries. When I want to change things on my own, help me to pause and pray for discernment. I know that you want me to utilize my creative talents and abilities fully, but then to surrender and leave the outcome up to You. It's hard, and I will falter, but I am learning to trust You. In Jesus' name, amen.

---

108 John Ortberg, *The Me I Want To Be: The Me I Want to Be: Becoming God's Best Version of You* (Grand Rapids: Zondervan, 2009), 64.
109 Ortberg, 66.

65. HAPPINESS IN THE MIDST OF DIFFICULT TIMES

Psalm 68:3. *But let the righteous be joyful; let them exult before God; let them be jubilant with joy.*

Happiness is elusive, fleeting, and hard to define. Everyone wants to be happy, but it seems that the harder we try to be happy, the more it escapes us. Eugene Peterson asserts that you can't manufacture happiness or will it to occur. Even worse, when you depend on the world to define happiness, you are quickly led to acquiring "things" and taking from another to satisfy yourself. Instead, follow Christ's example and realize that it is more blessed to give than to receive; more rewarding to have a servant-attitude and help others. As we learn to give and share, our vitality increases, and we may experience happiness. It is not a guarantee—experiencing joy is probably a better word for the Christian (see Reflection 15), but happiness is possible and can come when we least expect it—even amid our difficult times. Family times can be happy times when we realize how fortunate we are to have other people to be close to and to relate to. Yes, there is family strife, too, and "difficult" relatives, but, in the grand scheme of things, we are fortunate to have a family. I am currently blessed with four grandchildren, and they are a frequent source of happiness as I watch them grow and play and interact. (And when they get difficult, I always have the grandparent's prerogative of returning them back to their parents!) Another source of happiness is to behold God's creation: enjoy a walk in the park or the mountains or the seashore. You will invariably become aware of the magnificence of God's Kingdom. But, happiness is not an external event; it occurs when we are inwardly aware of God's blessing. As Peterson points out, "[Happiness is] not a matter of having a good day, not an occasional run of luck. It is an 'inner strength of the soul . . . the vital power, without which no living being can exist."[110] And that "vital power" is none other than Christ Himself who has come to show us and to help us live a life full of faith and exuberance with purpose. Yes, despite our difficult circumstances, we always have something

---

110 Eugene H. Peterson, *A Long Obedience in the Same Direction: Discipleship in an Instant Society* (Downers Grove: InterVarsity Press, 1980), 113.

to be thankful for—we are blessed, and the source of that blessing is Christ, in whom we place our trust, in whom we experience the joy of Christian living and on occasion, happiness.

PRAYER: Dear Lord, Thank You for my many blessings. When I reflect on them, I am grateful to You, and, when I realize that in and through You I can live a life full of faith and exuberance with purpose, I am happy. Not always, but happy enough to rely on You to sustain my life. In Jesus' name, amen.

66. GIVING THE HOLY SPIRIT CREDIT[111]

Galatians 5:22-23a. *The fruit of the Spirit is love, joy, peace, patience, kindness, generosity, faithfulness, gentleness, and self control.*

Sometimes I don't think we give the Holy Spirit enough credit. It is after all, Christ's presence inside us inspiring us to see heavenly possibilities in earthly circumstances. The Holy Spirit gives us glimpses into the heavenly realm, that overlapping, interlocking sphere where God's will is perfectly done. Henry Nouwen even goes so far as to say, "In and through the Spirit of Christ, we become others' Christs living in all places and at all times. In and through the Spirit, we come to know all that Jesus knew, and we are able to do all that he did."[112] That is an amazing statement; to think that through the Spirit we can be everything that Christ did and knew while He was among us. But, if it is "[not I], but it is Christ who lives in me" (Galatians 2:20), what else are we to expect? Nothing short of being Christ—but only through God's gift of the Holy Spirit. And, only when we relinquish our own egos and desires to control everything on our own. Through the Spirit, we don't just try to imitate Jesus, but rather to be transformed into living christs. We can recognize this transformation by its fruits: love, joy, peace, patience, kindness, goodness, truthfulness, gentleness, and self-control. Do you see how this awareness of the power of the Holy Spirit can help you deal with your difficult time? Stop struggling so much and avail yourself of a power that is beyond you (and at the same time, within you).

PRAYER: Dear Lord, Help me to give more credit to the Spirit and the fruits of the Spirit. It is nothing short of Christ living in me, which is rather astonishing to contemplate, and can be realized only by relinquishing my self-control and abandoning myself to faith and the work of the Holy Spirit in my life. Help me to give the Spirit more credit for helping me navigate the trials and tribulations of life. In Jesus' name, amen.

---

111 Henri Nouwen, *The Selfless Way of Christ: Downward Mobility and the Spiritual Life* (London: Darton, Longman and Todd, 2007), 41-43; Portions paraphrased.
112 Nouwen, 42.

67. DON'T LOOK FOR THE "QUICK FIX"[113]

2 Peter 3:9. *The Lord is not slow about his promise, as some think of slowness, but is patient with you, not wanting any to perish, but all to come to repentance.*

We are all about instant gratification these days. We want the quick fix, the solution to our problems in thirty seconds (the length of time it takes to sell you something via a TV commercial). Eugene Peterson asserts that unfortunately, many people treat their religion that way, too. Give it to me in short spurts, in quick doses, maybe at a retreat, possibly at the special services held during Christmas and Easter. But, don't bore me with the weekly routine of going to Sunday School and church each week. Oh, no, I'm much too busy for that. But, our faith journey isn't a sprint—it is what develops over the long haul. Discipleship is learning about Jesus little by little; savoring each tidbit, and then moving on after you have digested it. The word 'disciple' says "we are people who spend our lives apprenticed to our master, Jesus Christ. We are in a growing-learning relationship always. A disciple is a learner, but not in the academic setting of a schoolroom, rather at the work site of a craftsman. We do not acquire information about God, but skills on faith."[114] So, in your difficult time, don't look for the 'quick fix'. Spend time in the Scriptures and with ancient and contemporary Christian authors and devotionals. "Seek ye first the kingdom of God" (Matthew 6:33 KJV). There is no instant reward, either out of your difficulty or deeper into your faith. But, there is reward for the long haul.

PRAYER: Dear Lord, Give me a perspective for the long haul, not the 'quick fix'. Don't let me fall into the worldly trap that everything can be solved quickly. Give me the patience and the desire to study Your Word and learn Your craftsmanship over time. In Jesus' name, amen.

---

113   Eugene H. Peterson, *A Long Obedience in the Same Direction: Discipleship in an Instant Society* (Downers Grove: InterVarsity Press, 1980), 13-15; Portions paraphrased.
114   Peterson, 13.

68. CONTINUAL PRAYER[115]

Hebrews 13:15. *Through him, then, let us continually offer a sacrifice of praise to God, that is, the fruit of lips that confess his name.*

God is always present and aware of our goings on and our thoughts. That's how we can "pray continually" to Him—by being aware that all our thoughts are heard by Him. But, John Ortberg points out an interesting consideration as to why God seems to be absent sometimes in our lives: we act differently when we are in the presence of someone and talking about that person versus those times when we are not.[116] You probably say very different things about your mother-in-law to your acquaintances when you are alone with them as opposed to the time you know she is within earshot. So it is with God. God allows us to sometimes feel as if we are away from Him because He doesn't want people to give "forced compliance" without expressing their hearts. So, God makes it possible, in enormous love, for us to live as if He were not there. Then, when we pray, we put Him back into our minds. Of course, that is not the ultimate goal. We instead should attempt to live all our lives and speak all our words in the joyful awareness of the presence of God. Don't worry, He won't lash out if He hears something uncomfortable (perhaps unlike our mother-in-law). He has heard it all. But, as we become more and more aware of His minute by minute presence with us, and His unconditional love for us, we are ready to speak all our words in the joyful awareness of His presence. May it be so for you.

PRAYER: Dear Lord, In my difficult time, I may act and speak as though You are not present. Thank You for giving me that gift so that I am not unconsciously always trying to seek favor from You or to please You in some deceptive way. But the fact is, You are always present, and, as I grow, I can joyfully submit all my conversations to You in "continual prayer" and bathe myself in Your unconditional love. In Jesus' name, amen.

---

115 John Ortberg, *The Me I Want to Be: Becoming God's Best Version of You* (Grand Rapids: Zondervan, 2009), 132-135; Portions paraphrased.
116 Ortberg, 133-134.

69. A LITTLE BIT OF GOD GOES A LONG WAY[117]

Matthew 13:31-32. He put before them another parable: "The kingdom of heaven is like a mustard seed that someone took and sowed in his field; it is the smallest of all the seeds, but when it has grown it is the greatest of shrubs and becomes a tree, so that the birds of the air come and make nests in its branches."

Christian hope must be grounded in the now, not in the future. It must be sufficient to know that "the bride is present and that is enough reason for a foundational happiness, even if all else is falling apart."[118] We can't be consumed with thinking about tomorrow—waiting for a better day. Today may be all we have. Look right now for a tiny bit of God: a mustard seed, finding one lost coin, recovering one sheep like in Jesus' parables. A little bit of God goes a long way when you aren't putting off looking for Him tomorrow or the next day in hopes that He will give you something "better." It is in discovering the little daily blessings that life unfolds and has meaning. We waste so much of it looking to the day when we will be truly "blessed" that we miss the blessing right in front of our nose. Just stop for a minute and find something to be thankful for. Right now. Despite your difficult time, there is a little blessing waiting to be discovered. "Even a small indicator of God is still an indicator of God—and therefore an indicator of reason, meaning and final joy. A little bit of God goes a long way."[119]

PRAYER: Dear Lord, I must admit, even a little bit of You goes a long way. I spend so much time looking for the "big blessing," the "big break," the significant "thing" in my life that's going to transform me that I miss the little blessings that constitute life. And, when I take notice of the little things, the big things will fall into place without my trying to force them to happen or waiting for a "better day." Here is the thing, right now, that I am thankful for: _____. In Jesus' name, amen.

---

117 Richard Rohr, *Hope Against Darkness: The Transforming Vision of Saint Francis in an Age of Anxiety* (Cincinnati: St. Anthony Messenger Press, 2001), 1855-1859; Portions paraphrased.
118 Rohr, 1855.
119 Rohr, 1859; Earlier portions of this reflection paraphrased from this section of the book.

70. YOUR REWARD IN HEAVEN[120]

Matthew 10:42. *And whoever gives even a cup of cold water to one of these little ones in the name of a disciple—truly I tell you, none of these will lose their reward.*

A lot of people think that the way you are rewarded in heaven is by doing a lot of good things here on earth. It's like a "checkbox in the sky" where, when you come to judgment, Jesus ticks off all the good things you have done and rewards you accordingly. It implies that there is a hierarchy in heaven that is established by your good works. No way. We know that good works do not get us into heaven (Ephesians 2:8-10), so why should it be a basis for rewarding us in heaven? N.T. Wright has helped me out of this dilemma. Reward in the context of the New Testament means that the efforts we have undertaken now will be enhanced and magnified beyond our wildest dreams. "The 'reward' is *organically connected to the activity,* not some kind of arbitrary 'pat on the back', otherwise unrelated to the work that was done. And it is always far in abundance beyond any sense of direct or equivalent payment."[121] It's like practicing your golf swing so that you can play your best round of golf or learning to read so you can master the classics. What we learn to do here and now *counts,* and not only counts, but also will be enhanced and magnified beyond our wildest imagination in the Kingdom to come (like getting a score of eighteen on an eighteen-hole golf course!). I hope that this is a source of comfort to you as you go through your difficult time. Your efforts are not in vain—press on.

PRAYER: Dear Lord, It is a comfort to know that what I do here on earth counts for the future Kingdom—not as a set of "brownie points" that I accumulate, but rather to be enhanced and built upon in ways that I can't imagine. Help me to press on in the hope that all will be set right in Your Kingdom. In Jesus' name, amen.

---

120 N.T. Wright, *Surprised by Hope: Rethinking Heaven, the Resurrection, and the Mission of the Church* (New York: HarperOne, 2008), 160-164; Portions paraphrased.

121 Wright, 162.

71. USE YOUR CREATIVITY[122]

Ephesians 6:7-8. *Render service with enthusiasm, as to the Lord and not to men and women, knowing that whatever good we do, we will receive the same again from the Lord, whether we are slaves or free.*

Since everything we do here and now counts for the Kingdom, we need to reconsider what it means to be a servant of Christ. Of course, we should endeavor to improve the condition of the world as we find it through moral integrity, social consciousness, justice-seeking, and peacemaking. But there is more! We need to use all our God-given creative talents to glorify God. That means being creative through writing, poetry, art, music, and in other artistic ways. It's not a waste of time! It is practicing that which you love to do, in recognition that you will be rewarded in the Kingdom to come with amazing gifts, *based on what you have started now,* that you only dreamed you would be able to do! N.T. Wright likens it to sculpting a chalice now, which is then filled with the most incredible wine. It is a worthwhile endeavor to create the chalice, but an amazing reward to taste all the beauty and benefit of the chalice when it is put to its ultimate use. So, develop a hobby, become "artsy-craftsy," sing your heart out, learn to play an instrument, or write that novel that is inside you. It enhances the Kingdom now and will be multiplied in its effect in the Kingdom to come in ways we can't even imagine.

PRAYER: Dear Lord, I hadn't thought that developing my God given creative talents now has implications far beyond their current use. They bring glory to Your Kingdom now and will be built upon in the most amazing, unimaginable ways in the Kingdom to come. Despite the difficult time I am going through, help me to learn new ways of expressing my artistic side. It will bring pleasure to me and others now and create quite a "Wow!" factor in the Kingdom to come. In Jesus' name, amen.

---

122 N.T. Wright, *Surprised by Hope: Rethinking Heaven, the Resurrection, and the Mission of the Church* (New York: HarperOne, 2008), 161-162; Portions paraphrased.

72. PLUNGING INTO THE REALITY OF THE SITUATION[123]

1 Corinthians 7:24. *In whatever condition you were called, brothers and sisters, there remain with God.*

I keep harping on the importance of living in the moment (see Reflection 82). We tend to be anxious about the future or guilty about the past. Instead, James Martin, SJ, suggests that God's will is simply what He sends us *each day* in the way of circumstances, places, people, and problems (yes, *problems*). Instead of trying to figure out God's will as though we have a crystal ball, we can see that His will for us is clearly revealed in every situation of every day. He is the being with the crystal ball; if only we could learn to view all things as He sees them and sends them to us—daily. "God invites us to accept the inescapable realities placed in front of us. We can either turn away from that acceptance of life and continue on our own, or we can plunge into the 'reality of the situation' and try to find God there in new ways."[124] This is not the first time I've made this point, but it bears repeating: God is intersecting with our life most vividly in the here and now. The mundane, day-in to day-out process of living is the source of knowledge and wisdom to those souls who see God's purpose revealed in the here and now. It is not always a pleasant here and now (as you can attest in your difficult circumstances), but it is revealing and ultimately rewarding.

PRAYER: Dear Lord, I admit that I have an easier time escaping into future thoughts or dwelling in the past rather than living in the moment. Help me to see that the here and now is "where it's at." It is sufficient to live out what God sends me each day rather than to try to figure out the future. Even if the present is looking dim, it is teaching me something valuable. Thank You for giving me a present reality upon which to base my life. In Jesus' name, amen.

---

123 James Martin, SJ, *The Jesuit Guide to (Almost) Everything: A Spirituality for Real Life* (New York: HarperCollins, 2010), 281-283; Portions paraphrased.
124 Martin, SJ, 283.

73. LIVING IN THE MYSTERY[125]

Ephesians 1:9. *He has made known to us the mystery of his will, according to his good pleasure that he set forth in Christ.*

So, what do we mean by "humility?" Ilia Delio discussing St. Bonaventure puts it well: "By 'humility' Bonaventure meant a self-knowledge grounded in truth, patience with others, simplicity of life, attentive listening to others, courage to overcome temptations and a compassionate heart."[126] But, is it a stretch to give these attributes to God? Or, can we say that because we are manifesting God in our lives, and God lives in us, then God must be that way? Just look to Christ and consider it a mystery. God is a mystery of humble love, silence, and intimacy. It is a mystery that you cannot reason or try to figure out. You must simply live in the mystery. Love is a good summary of who God is and reinforces the mystery: When you love someone, you know him in a deeper way; yet, the more you know someone the less you truly know him. The more the face of the Lover is revealed, the more it is concealed. The overarching comfort in all of this is that God is incomprehensible and ineffable, far beyond our wildest imaginations, yet nearer to each of us than we are to ourselves. I hope that the magnificence of God and His intimacy is a comfort to you in your difficult time. He cannot be perceived by logic alone but through the pathway of the heart, silence, and love.

PRAYER: Dear Lord, I am overwhelmed by Your love for me. I cannot ever even think of it in logical terms, but rather perceive it through my love for You. You are grander than I can imagine, yet as close as my next breath. What a wonderful mystery! Let me marvel at the blessings You bestow upon this world. May it help me through my difficult circumstances. In Jesus' name, amen.

---

125   Ilia Delio, *The Humility of God: A Franciscan Perspective* (Cincinnati: St. Anthony Messenger Press, 2011), Kindle, 280-290; Portions paraphrased.
126   Delio, 287.

74. MAKING A DIFFERENCE[127]

Matthew 28:18. *And Jesus came and said to them, "All authority in heaven and on earth has been given to me."*

In your difficult time, aren't there instances when you question whether Christ is in control of the cosmos here and now? Some believers think that His rule doesn't begin until His second coming. But, when He ascended into heaven, Christ acknowledged, "All authority on heaven and earth has been given to me" (Matthew 28:18). Heaven is the "control room" for earth, governed by Christ and enabled by His followers. Things are a mess right now because evil and death are still present. It's like the D-Day invasion in World War 2. After D-Day, the Allies knew that victory was a certainty, but they still had a lot of work and "cleaning up" ahead of them. So it is with the Kingdom. Although a major battle has been won (Christ's resurrection: "D-Day"), there is much work to be done before final victory is declared. And, we Christians are the ones commissioned to do the work—to seek moral and social justice, feed the poor and hungry, seek peace, and love our neighbor as ourselves. We won't be able to "fix" everything until Christ returns, but we can make a difference.

PRAYER: Dear Lord, Help me to make a difference. I know that I can't solve all the world's problems, only Christ can do that, and not until He returns. But, in the meantime, there is much to be done. I am Christ's ambassador here on earth, and He is accomplishing His work through me. It is a challenge but a blessing to help in this way. In Jesus' name, amen.

---

127 N.T. Wright, *Surprised by Hope: Rethinking Heaven, the Resurrection, and the Mission of the Church* (New York: HarperOne, 2008), 111; Portions paraphrased.

75. INTENTIONAL VS. SPONTANEOUS PRAYER

Matthew 6:6. *But whenever you pray, go into your room and shut the door and pray to your Father who is in secret; and your Father who sees in secret, will reward you.*

"Prayer, more than any other single activity, is what places us in the flow of the Spirit. When we pray, hearts get convicted, sin gets confessed, believers get united, intentions get encouraged, people receive guidance, the church is strengthened, stubbornness gets melted, wills get surrendered, evil gets defeated, grace gets released, illness gets healed, sorrows are comforted, faith is born, hope is grown, and love triumphs. In prayer—in the presence of God—we become closest to being fully ourselves."[128] I cherish my private times of prayer. I set aside two particular times: one just after breakfast and one just after dinner to spend time in prayer. I have a favorite place, my home office, and a favorite chair, my recliner, in the corner of the office to pray. And then, there is spontaneous prayer. Sometimes when we feel that we "have" to pray, it doesn't come as naturally as the times when we just "let go" and are aware of God's presence in our lives: that is a form of prayer. We just go outside alone and invite Jesus to come with us. We share with Him our observations about the goodness of His creation, or we talk to Him about something that is on our mind—your difficult time is a prime candidate right now. Cultivate your prayer time. Don't restrict it just to the prescribed times but be spontaneous and invite Him into the innermost parts of your being. You will come out refreshed and ready to take on life's problems.

PRAYER: Dear Lord, I value the times that I set aside intentionally to pray and meditate. And, I also value the times when I am spontaneous and invite You into the innermost parts of my life. When my mind wanders in prayer, help me to refocus. Maybe I just need a break and to find another time when it seems more natural to be with You. You are available 24/7 to hear me, comfort me, and encourage me. In Jesus' name, amen.

---

128 John Ortberg, *The Me I Want To Be: The Me I Want to Be: Becoming God's Best Version of You* (Grand Rapids: Zondervan, 2009), 180.

76. THE CYCLICAL PROCESS OF FAITH[129]

John 12:46. *I have come as light into the world, so that everyone who believes in me should not remain in the darkness.*

There is a cyclical process that God uses to bring us closer to Him. There is a springtime of our spiritual life when prayer is easy and when we have great energy to pursue various forms of social service. We trust God; we enjoy a certain freedom from our vices; we feel a sense of satisfaction with our spiritual endeavors. But then, God pulls the rug out from under us. He is inviting us to a new level of self-knowledge that can be found only by going down. We are plunged in darkness, spiritual dryness, and confusion. Perhaps this is where you are in your difficult time. We think that God has abandoned us. But eventually, there comes a period of peace, enjoyment of a new inner-freedom as we gain insight from our period of darkness. We have a new perspective on life and God that would not have been available to us had we not gone through the darkness. All of this takes time—it is a blessing that it does not happen suddenly, so that we can handle it. There is an impermanence to this process. Just when we think that we have gotten ahold of new spiritual direction and insight, the darkness comes again. And here is the thought to hold onto: the period of darkness, the time when we are at the bottom of the pile of our emotional debris, is the time that we are in divine union with God. There is no other obstacle to our closeness to Him.

PRAYER: Dear Lord, I guess I should be thankful for these periods of darkness when You seem to be absent in my life because they are a springboard to new spiritual insight, but it's hard. I don't like the lonely times, the difficult times, and the feeling that You just don't care. Thank God that there is a cycle to all of this and that there is growth and the promise of heightened awareness of Your grace. Help me to see the darkness as a time of divine union with You. In Jesus' name, amen.

---

129 Thomas Keating, *The Daily Reader for Contemplative Living: Excerpts from the Works of Father Thomas Keating* (New York: Continuum, 2006), 179; Concepts drawn from the book.

77. FEAR AS A MOTIVATOR IN LIFE[130]

Matthew 14:27. *But immediately Jesus spoke to them and said, "Take heart, it is I; do not be afraid."*

Do you realize how much of what you do is done out of fear? We fear losing our job, money, reputation, or prestige. We are so concerned with self-image and "looking good" or "appearing proper" that we lose sight and live our life out of fear, not love. We tend to see everything through our egocentric agenda: "How will this make me look?," "How will this inconvenience me?," "How will this make me feel?" The worldly system depends on this fear motivation to promulgate its existence. We are rewarded (or punished) by the degree to which we buy into the system. As you move into more of a contemplative lifestyle, you begin to "clear the lens" of self-absorption and see things from a different perspective—a perspective that sees humanity just a little less than God (Psalm 8:5) and discerns that life is bigger than just our individual contribution. There is a "river of life"; a flow of the Spirit that encompasses so much more. We see that things are as they are regardless of whether we like them or not, or how we perceive them. "The mystery is to receive things just as they are and be ready to let them teach us."[131] So, the right question to ask in your difficult time is, "What are you trying to teach me Lord, in this experience?" rather than, "Why is this happening to me?" The right motivation is love not fear, trying to please a world system of rewards and punishment, but recognizing that we are cherished beings in God's eyes. This change in perspective will make a big difference in your life.

PRAYER: Dear Lord, I didn't realize how much fear is a motivator in my life. This mode of life has been so ingrained in me that I haven't considered that there is a better way. Help me to grasp the breadth and depth of Your love, and to see myself as a child of God rather than a victim of the system. I know now to try to understand what my difficult time is trying to teach me, rather than to wallow in self-pity and fear. Let Your unconditional love surround me and overcome my fears. In Jesus' name, amen.

---

130   Thomas Keating, *The Daily Reader for Contemplative Living: Excerpts from the Works of Father Thomas Keating* (New York: Continuum, 2006), Portions paraphrased.
131   Richard Rohr, *Everything Belongs: The Gift of Contemplative Prayer* (New York: Crossroad, 2003), 90.

78. THE CHAOS OF FAITH[132]

Matthew 7:26. *And everyone who hears these words of mine and does not act on them will be like a foolish man who built his house on sand.*

There is an interesting interplay between relying on established norms and what Richard Rohr calls "the chaos of faith."[133] On the one hand, we want to be grounded in norms and tradition. We attend church; we follow a litany; we read Scripture; we pray. But that is not enough for the creativity and carving out of a new future that God desires. To achieve that requires a certain abandonment; a "letting go" of norms and striking out in new directions—acknowledging that there is a certain chaos to life that is healthy. If everything were a sure thing life would be boring indeed—too predictable. Instead, we can look to each day as a gift: wrapped in the certainty of God's unconditional love and mercy towards us, but with a surprise inside called "life." We are free to loosen the shackles of everyday norms and create new and beautiful ways to demonstrate our love for God. Are you too tradition-bound? Has your difficult time put you in a box that is too confining and restrictive? Cut loose! Try something new! Don't be afraid to let a little chaos into your life. Underneath are the everlasting arms—you are in good hands, and you have lots of latitude to let your creative juices flow on the Lord's behalf.

PRAYER: Dear Lord, I like my traditions, but sometimes they box me in. Help me to embrace some chaos in my life and, through it, be more creative. Life is too short to live it prescriptively all the time. You have provided space for me to cut loose and try new things. Thank You for the opportunity to live with uncertainty while at the same time knowing that You have my best interests at heart. In Jesus' name, amen.

---

132 Richard Rohr, *Hope Against Darkness: The Transforming Vision of Saint Francis in an Age of Anxiety* (Cincinnati: St. Anthony Messenger Press, 2001), 1800-1835; Portions paraphrased.
133 Rohr, 1831.

79. THE THIRD WAY[134]

Ephesians 1:17. *I pray that the God of our Lord Jesus Christ, the Father of glory, may give you a spirit of wisdom and revelation as you come to know him.*

I wish that I could adequately convey the concept of paradox in our spiritual life. We sometimes think that the spiritual life is "getting away from it all" like the monks do—escaping reality by reflecting on an "otherworldly" existence that is beautiful to conceptualize but doesn't exist in reality. Then, there is the all-too-real coming to terms with life in this world, with its pulls and pushes for our affections and allegiances, and its appeal to our ego and dependence on the rewards and punishments of world systems. Both worlds must exist in tension with one another—that is the paradox. An analogy is Jesus, Himself, who would go into the desert to get away from the worldly pressures facing Him, but then return to the city to get involved in the day-to-day aspects of humanity. The desert represents our spiritual life—a life of detachment from the day-to-day grind. The city represents our soul life—a life of attachment to the things of this world—our relationships, our day-to-day struggles; the things of life. This tension between attachment and detachment is sometimes called the Third Way.[135] "In the Third Way, we stand in the middle, neither taking the world on from the power position nor denying it for fear of the pain it will bring. We hold the realization, seeing the dark side of reality and the pain of the world, but we hold it until it transforms us, knowing that we are complicit in the evil and also complicit in the holiness. Once we stand in that third spacious way, neither fighting nor fleeing, we are in the place of grace out of which newness comes."[136] It is a place of wisdom; it is a place of creativity; it is a place of release. Try to learn to live in this dance between attachment and detachment. It will put your difficult time in proper perspective and bring you closer to God.

---

134 Richard Rohr, *Everything Belongs: The Gift of Contemplative Prayer* (New York: Crossroad, 2003), 170-173; Portions paraphrased.
135 Rohr, 171.
136 Rohr, 171.

PRAYER: Dear Lord, I see the paradox: life is full of pressure to succeed and make money and be "successful"—full of "attachments." But, there is another side, usually found in my prayer life, of detachment and awareness that there is something beyond my day-to-day existence that is very appealing and hints that there is another dimension to life that I can't even see: my spiritual life. Help me to see that both attachment and detachment are operating in my life, and that I can live well if I acknowledge this paradox and live creatively within it. In Jesus' name, amen.

80. BEING MASTERED BY THE SPIRIT

Luke 12:36. *Be like those who are waiting for their master to return from the wedding banquet, so that they may open the door for him as soon as he comes and knocks.*

Henri Nouwen has a wonderful statement to ponder: "The discipline of the Christian disciple is not to master anything, but rather to be mastered by the Spirit. True Christian discipline is the human effort to create the space in which the Spirit of Christ can transform us into his lineage."[137] Most of us work hard at mastering our faith instead of opening ourselves up to the work of the Holy Spirit. But, that is not to say that there aren't disciplines that are healthy for your faith and your relationship with God. Nouwen cites three:

1. **The discipline of the church**. This is the place where we come to understand and live out the Christ-event, through liturgy and worship. The "event" is that we, as Christians, represent the living Christ in time and space. As we go through Christmas and Easter and Pentecost and the seasons of the church year, we begin to understand that our story reveals itself through the story of Christ.

2. **The discipline of the Book**. We read the Word and let it soak into the most hidden corners of our being. "Among the many texts the church presents to us each year, there might be one word, one story, one parable, one sentence that has the power to turn us around, to change our whole life, to give us a new heart and new mind, to conform us to Christ.[138]

3. **The discipline of the Heart**. The discipline of the heart is the discipline of personal prayer, which, according to Nouwen, leads us not just to our own heart, but to the heart of God. Prayer is a willingness to be alone with God. "To truly become men and women whose identities are hidden in God, we need to have the courage to enter empty-handed into the place of solitude."[139] In your difficult time, take heed

---

137 Henri Nouwen, *The Selfless Way of Christ: Downward Mobility and the Spiritual Life* (London: Darton, Longman and Todd, 2007), 70.
138 Nouwen, 78.
139 Nouwen, 85.

to follow these recommended disciplines: the church, the Book, and the Heart. You will begin the process of recovery and contentment.

PRAYER: Dear Lord, Help me to "create the space" where the Spirit can transform me. I am guilty of working hard at my faith, rather than opening myself up to the workings of the Spirit. But, these are helpful disciplines that are discussed to help me in my journey. I commit myself to practicing them. In Jesus' name, amen.

81. TRIUMPH OF GRACE

Philippians 3:14. *I press on toward the goal for the prize of the heavenly call of God in Christ Jesus.*

Thomas Keating talks about three stages of a project which we go through again and again that are led by the Holy Spirit. First, we take on some great project, full of resolve and energy. We may feel called by God to take on this project, and it may at first go very well for us and appear to be a huge success. But then, our initial success fails or disappoints in some way. Things don't ultimately turn out as we expected. We encounter a difficult time. We are disappointed and let down. We feel like the whole project was a huge mistake, and we are sorry that we even took it on—and we resolve never to take on so large an endeavor again. Sometime later, there is a triumph of grace; often totally unexpected. We gain new insight from our experience, or suddenly an aspect that we thought was lost is found and renewed. Something good comes out of our seemingly failed effort. We are encouraged to try again. In your difficult time, be patient and look for this triumph of grace. It will come in an unexpected way. It will surprise and encourage you. It will remind you that God is in control after all. Then, you will be willing to take on something new, and start the cycle all over again.

PRAYER: Dear Lord, I await the "triumph of grace." It is hard being in the valley and being patient at the same time. But sometimes I get glimpses of hope—a feeling that not all is lost and that You care. Sometimes, it is in the encouraging words of a friend; sometimes a moment during worship or alone with nature; sometimes when I pray. These glimpses sustain me. I become aware of the goodness of life and that You love each and every one of us in the circumstances we are in, and that Your grace will carry us along. In Jesus' name, amen.

82. EXPERIENCING THE 'NOW' OF LIFE

Romans 12:2. *Do not be conformed to this world, but be transformed by the renewing of your minds, so that you may discern what is the will of God—what is good and acceptable and perfect.*

I've been reading lately about how important it is to live in the present moment, to experience the "now" of life.[140] I have learned that the mind does not live in the now.[141] It is too busy thinking about the future or past. So how do we live in the "now"? One important way is to meditate. I use the method of centering prayer (see Reflection 20). But, recently, I heard another definition of living in the present moment that made sense to me. "When we are present, we hear the superego's voice but do not give it any energy; the 'all-powerful' voice then becomes just another aspect of the moment."[142] The superego is our inner voice that rewards us when we do what pleases it and admonishes us when we do something that it disapproves of. According to Don Richard Riso, "the superego is the 'internalized voice' of our parents and other authority figures, both old and new."[143] So, to live more in the present, consider your internal voice as just another input that you acknowledge but don't allow to control you—it becomes "another aspect of the moment." Incredible things begin to happen when you learn to live this way—you are more spiritually aware; your problems and difficult time are seen in the proper perspective, as part of the Big Picture that is greater than you and is guiding you. You may not be able to live like this all the time, but the times you do are sufficient to sustain you.

PRAYER: Dear Lord, It is hard to live in the "now." I have so many thoughts and fears. But now that I realize it is possible for the mind to live in the "now," and that my inner voice (my 'superego') does not have to be all-powerful, but, rather, another aspect of the moment, I am calmer. I see that I am part of something greater than myself and that it is good—Your creation and the wonderful gift of life speak to me in beautiful ways. Thank You for my new insights. In Jesus' name, amen.

---

140 See, for example, Richard Rohr, *The Naked Now*.
141 Richard Rohr, *A Lever and A Place to Stand: The Contemplative Stance, The Active Prayer* (New York: Paulist Press, 2011), 11.
142 Don Richard Riso and Russ Hudson, *The Wisdom of the Enneagram* (New York: Bantam, 1999), 354.
143 Riso and Hudson, 352.

83. SELF IMPORTANCE VS. HUMILITY[144]

Romans 7:18. *For I know that nothing good dwells within me, that is, in my flesh [ego]. I can will what is right, but I cannot do it.*

I can't say too much about how pride and our ego get in the way of enjoying life. We think that by controlling everything, we can carve out our own happiness, rather than realizing that we are dependent beings whose chief glory is to reflect God's brilliance. The word for this dependency on God for our sustenance is "humility." Test your humility by seeing how you would react in these circumstances[145]:

- When you are around other people, do you insist on promoting your opinions, driving home your points and being the last one to talk on an issue?

- How do you feel about the driver who cuts you off on the freeway? Are you shocked by his insensitivity to your rights as a driver? Or how do you feel about the family which grabs the restaurant table that you had eyed for yourself?

- How do you treat others? How do you relate to the person taking your order at the fast food restaurant drive-through window? Or how do you interact with the cashier at the local convenience store?

You get the idea. Sometimes we are so focused on the difficulties we are going through that we aren't very humble or accommodating of others. Our own self-importance gets in the way. Instead, try to look at things from the other person's point-of-view, and be happy when things go their way, not jealous because it didn't happen to you. There is plenty that will come your way, too, so don't be stingy. "If you're so busy clawing and scratching for every blessing you can squeeze out of life, you won't have time to appreciate the blessings that others receive. Lighten up, loosen up, and find ways to

---

144 John Michael Talbot, *The Lessons of St. Francis: How to Bring Simplicity and Spirituality into Your Daily Life* (New York: Dutton, 1997), 87-89; Portions paraphrased.
145 Talbot, 87; As listed.

appreciate everyone else's uniqueness and giftedness without viewing this as some kind of criticism of you and the way you are."[146]

PRAYER: Dear Lord, I recognize times when I fail to be humble. And, I see how humility can lead to a better outlook on life. Rather than be so concerned about myself, I can have the freedom to welcome the blessings that go to others knowing that my turn will come. Help me to be humbler. In Jesus' name, amen.

---

146 Talbot, 89.

84. RELATIONSHIPS

1 Samuel 20:4. *Then Jonathan said to David, "Whatever you say, I will do for you."*

It is difficult to "go it alone." God made us to be in relationship to one another. The distinction between truly happy people and not so happy people is the breadth and depth of their relationships. This is especially true when you're going through a difficult time. Your relationships need to be more than surface acquaintances. You need to have people you can count on; that you can confide in; who are "there for you." John Ortberg asks the following questions to see if you are where you need to be regarding relationships.[147] You should be able to answer most of these questions with a "yes," or else start seeking ways to strengthen your relationships:

- When something goes wrong, do you have at least one friend you can easily talk to?

- Do you have a friend that you can drop in on at any time without calling ahead?

- Is there someone who can accurately name your greatest fears and temptations?

- Do you have one or more friends with whom you meet with regularly?

- Do you have a friend you know well enough to trust their confidentiality?

- If you received good news like a promotion, do you have a friend who you would call immediately just to let them know?

If you struggled to find "yes" answers to many of the above questions, then consider joining a small group or inviting someone out for a coffee as a start in strengthening your relationships.

PRAYER: Dear Lord, I know having strong relationships goes a long way toward helping me cope with my difficult situation. Thank You for [name specific persons in your life that you are thankful for]. Help me to be deliberate in cultivating strong relationships by reaching out to others and loving them. In Jesus' name, amen.

---

147 John Ortberg, *The Me I Want to Be: Becoming God's Best Version of You* (Grand Rapids: Zondervan, 2009), 193.

85. COMPASSION[148]

Matthew 9:36. *When he saw the crowds, he had compassion for them, because they were harassed and helpless, like sheep without a shepherd.*

Compassion is dropping your guard and seeing the pain of others, hearing their cries of need and reaching out to them in love and blessing. In short, it is seeing Christ in others—in "the least of these." A good method to increase your capacity to be compassionate is to actively listen to those with whom you interact. Don't judge or criticize, just listen and be empathetic. "Compassion isn't about whether you approve or disapprove of what someone is saying; it's about understanding another person. It isn't about promoting your agenda; it's about comprehending someone else's."[149] Of course, the "acid test" of compassion is in how you treat those who are worse off than you. You may think that you are compassionate, as long as you don't have to deal with the homeless person looking for a handout, or the street person that reeks of alcohol asking you for a dollar. Can you put yourself in his/her shoes? "There but for the grace of God go I."[150] It was why Mother Teresa was so compassionate, and why we have a ways to go. She saw Christ in everyone. As Frederick Buechner says, "[Compassion] is the knowledge that there can never really be any peace and joy for me until there is peace and joy finally for you too."[151] It's all about wanting the best for one another, or as Jesus would say, "loving your neighbor as yourself." You discover that despite your difficult time, there are others who deserve your compassion and love. We are all in this together.

PRAYER: Dear Lord, Please help me to be more compassionate by listening more actively to others going through a difficult time and seeing the best in people that I might not normally associate with. We are all in this together, and we can help each other cope with life's difficulties by being more compassionate and understanding of each other's troubles. In Jesus' name, amen.

---

148 John Michael Talbot, *The Lessons of St. Francis: How to Bring Simplicity and Spirituality into Your Daily Life* (New York: Dutton, 1997), 163; Portions paraphrased.
149 Talbot, 152-154.
150 Phrase first spoken by the English evangelical preacher and martyr, John Bradford (1510-1555).
151 Talbot, 154; The author quoting Frederick Buechner.

86. MAKING DECISIONS[152]

Acts 16:4. *As they went from town to town, they delivered to them for observance the decisions that had been reached by the apostles and elders who were in Jerusalem.*

Do you have difficulty making decisions? The Jesuits have a three-step process that you may find helpful. The first step is the "no-brainer" decision where there is no doubt in your mind what to do. The second step requires some deliberation. Pray about it and choose the path that gives you greater consolation—a sense of God's presence and a feeling of peace and "rightness" about the choice. The flip side is desolation, where you feel uneasy, restless, listless, tepid, or unhappy—avoid decisions that lead you to desolation. The third step is the most difficult: you find yourself with two or more good alternatives, but neither one is the obvious choice. There are two methods suggested for this type of decision. The first is to reason it out. It is important to start with indifference about the alternatives (i.e., you don't have an emotional bias one way or the other). Then, pray about it, think about which alternative would most please God, list the possible positive and negative outcomes of each option in your head or on a piece of paper, pray again over the lists, and then seek some sort of confirmation—an endorsement from friends or relatives, or a feeling of consolation like we mentioned in step one. The second method is to use your imagination: imagine what advice you would give to another person who is trying to make the same decision. Or, more dramatically, imagine yourself at the point of death, or, at the Last Judgment, presenting your choice before God. A final piece of advice is to imagine what your "best self" would do. If I were a freer and more loving person, what would I do? Hopefully, these suggestions will help you with your decision-making process during your difficult time.

PRAYER: Dear Lord, Sometimes I have difficulty making decisions. I hope that using these three steps will help me make the right ones. Help me to develop a sense of consolation about what is right and to seek confirmation from others. In Jesus' name, amen.

---

152 James Martin, SJ, *The Jesuit Guide to (Almost) Everything: A Spirituality for Real Life* (New York: HarperCollins, 2010), 313-332; Portions paraphrased.

87. WORK IS GOOD[153]

Job 1:10b. *You have blessed the work of his hands, and his possessions have increased in the land.*

Perhaps boredom or loneliness is at the root of your difficult time. Consider a change in your work environment, or, if you are unemployed, actively seek work. Work is a good thing. God worked for six days before He rested on the seventh, and He sees merit in our creating value with our work. The trick is to find something to do that matches the level of skill we possess to the level of challenge before us. We should cultivate what we are good at and find work that utilizes that talent. If you haven't yet figured out what you are good at, John Ortberg suggests you read the book *Now Discover Your Strengths* by Buckingham and Clifton.[154] Once you know your strengths, you must find a fit in the kind of work you do. This is no easy task in an economy where jobs are hard to come by. But, it is worth the effort. The prize is to have a job where you are in the "flow": "you are so caught up in your work that time somehow seems to be altered; you are fully focused without having to work at it. You are being stretched and challenged but without a sense of stress or worry. You have a sense of engagement or oneness with what you are doing."[155] It's almost like being swept up by something greater than yourself. You experience "flow" best at work rather than leisure. It is purposeful yet effortless. Sounds too good to be true, doesn't it? But, many people experience it. You can too when you realize "we do not work mainly for money, recognition, promotion, applause, or fame. We work for flow. We live for flow. Flow is part of what we experience in that partnership with God, and God in turn uses flow to shape us."[156]

PRAYER: Dear Lord, I have a long way to go before I experience this "flow." But, it is refreshing to consider that work can be rewarding in this way. Help me to persevere in finding the right match between my strengths and level of challenge at work so I am fulfilled. In Jesus' name, amen.

---

153 John Ortberg, *The Me I Want to Be: Becoming God's Best Version of You* (Grand Rapids: Zondervan, 2009), 220-222; Portions paraphrased.
154 Ortberg, 220.
155 Ortberg, 221.
156 Ortberg, 222.

88. WORKING IN THE SPIRIT[157]

Genesis 24:19. When [Rebekah] had finished giving him a drink, she said, "I will draw for your camels also, until they have finished drinking."

"When we discover the gifts God has given us and the passions that engage us, and we put them to work in the service of values we deeply believe in—in conscious dependence on God—then we are working in the Spirit."[158] We are also likely living out our calling. There are jobs we do for money; there are jobs we do as a career; and then there are the jobs we do because they are a part of our calling. We do them for a higher purpose. The garbage collector is not just collecting trash, he is making the world a cleaner and safer place. The nurse does not just give injections and take blood; she improves the quality of life for her patients. It is a matter of perspective: one person's drudgery is another person's call. The Bible tells the story of a chief servant of Abraham, who was to select a wife for Abraham's son, Isaac (Genesis 4). The servant stopped for rest and was greeted by Rebekah, who offered to get water for him and all of his camels—that was a LOT of water! A thirsty camel can drink up to thirty gallons of water, and the servant had ten camels. She didn't do it because she knew that the servant might reward her with the prize of becoming Isaac's wife, she just did it because it was her call—to be a servant to those who thirsted along her pathway. And, of course, she was selected to be Isaac's wife and became a part of sacred history. So, no matter how small the job, do it with passion and commitment; do it as a call, and you will be rewarded. Probably not in the way Rebekah was rewarded but in some way that shows God's grace toward you.

PRAYER: Dear Lord, As I struggle through this difficult time, help me to see my job as a "call." Give me the perspective to see the grander side of my work, so that I can do it with passion and in the Spirit. I know now that work is an important part of my life and that You are pleased when we can abandon ourselves to our work and find satisfaction in it. May it be so for me. In Jesus' name, amen.

---

157 John Ortberg, *The Me I Want to Be: Becoming God's Best Version of You* (Grand Rapids: Zondervan, 2009), 225-227; Portions paraphrased.
158 Ortberg, 227.

89. ASPECTS OF PRAYER

Psalm 17:6. *I call upon you, for you will answer me, O God; incline your ear to me, hear my words.*

There's a world of difference between knowing *about* something and actually *knowing* something. Maybe you can build a boat and lecture about nautical history, but, if you've never set sail in the water, you haven't really experienced boating; you just know about it. Likewise, you might be able to describe in incredible detail the biographical information about Beethoven and explain how he wrote his music. But, if you've never wept while listening to the seventh symphony, you really don't know the man and his work.[159] The same goes for knowing God in prayer. You can study the Scriptures, read contemporary authors, give Sunday School lessons about Jesus, but, until you have experienced the fullness of God in your prayer life, you really don't know God. May we all experience the mystical union with God like Brother Boniface Macs talks about in *Franciscan Mysticism*: "The grace of God sometimes overflows like a river and invades the emotional power of the soul . . . there follows spiritual intoxication, which is a breaking out of overwhelming tenderness and delicious intimacies greater than the heart can desire or contain." In the midst of your difficult time, you may not be to that point in your prayer life yet but keep praying. Carve out a time to pray. Spend time in silence. Thank God for the blessings in your life. Make your prayers ones of searching, submission, and dependence, not ones where you just ask God for "stuff" or to help you out of a bind. And, of course, don't forget to intercede for others. Prayer is an act of love toward God and a significant blessing.

PRAYER: Dear Lord, I don't just want to know about You but to know You intimately. Help me in my prayer life to do the things recommended in this reflection and to cherish the times that I go to You in prayer. In Jesus' name, amen.

---

159 John Michael Talbot, *The Lessons of St. Francis: How to Bring Simplicity and Spirituality into Your Daily Life* (New York: Dutton, 1997), 228; These examples were taken from and portions of subsequent discussion in this reflection are paraphrased from the author.

90. WIRED FOR A CHALLENGE[160]

Numbers 13:30-31. But Caleb quieted the people before Moses, and said, "Let us go up at once and occupy it, for we are well able to overcome it." Then the men who had gone up with him said, "We are not able to go up against this people, for they are stronger than we."

"It is in working to solve problems and overcome challenges that we become the person God wants us to be."[161] Too often, we try to escape problems, to seek the comfortable way, to escape our difficult time, to take the easy way out. But, it is in facing challenges that we come alive. An example is the Biblical character Caleb, who, at the age of forty, scouted out the Promised Land and was one of only two who thought that the Jewish nation would be successful in conquering the land (Numbers 13). The Jews chickened out and spent another forty years in the wilderness. At the ripe old age of eighty, Caleb once again had the opportunity to volunteer for service to his compatriots in claiming the Promised Land. He volunteered for the toughest duty— to take the hill country, a more difficult battle than the flatlands. That is the attitude that God wants us to have—to take on the difficult assignment—a cause greater than ourselves so that we are dependent on God for success. So, rather than be discouraged by your difficult time, consider it a challenge! Recognize that without problems, life would be boring indeed—we are wired for a challenge. And, if your challenge seems to be too much for you, pray about it and turn it over to God. There is a way out of your dilemma, and God is on your side.

PRAYER: Dear Lord, Help me to see that I am wired for a challenge and that the difficulties I am experiencing can be overcome with Your help. Like Caleb, I can sign up for the challenge, not avoid it. By facing my difficulties head on, I model the life that You have chosen for us: far from boring, filled with excitement, and anything but dull. In Jesus' name, amen.

---

160 John Ortberg, *The Me I Want to Be: Becoming God's Best Version of You* (Grand Rapids: Zondervan, 2009), 243-245; Portions paraphrased.
161 Ortberg, 247.

91. THE GOD WHO IS[162]

Psalm 24:7. *Lift up your heads, O gates! and be lifted up, O ancient doors! that the King of glory may come in.*

Too often, we just want a God who gives, gives, gives, rather than a God who is, is, is. You wouldn't be best friends with a person just on the basis of what he can give you or do for you. You are best friends because of who he is—his character, his honesty, his devotion to a cause, his allegiance to you. So why is God any different? It is a *personal* relationship, based on mutual regard; not on what you can "get" from God, but on reflecting upon who God is and cherishing His love for you. Right now, during your difficult time, you may be focused more on the "get" side of your relationship rather than cultivating a personal relationship with God. Too often, your prayer life is filled with asking for "stuff" rather than a two-way conversation in which you express your gratitude for all blessings that God has bestowed upon you. You should humbly recognize that you are a sinner and don't really deserve all that God has given you, and then spend time in silence while God communes with you. I am an advocate of devoting long periods of time in silent meditation before God, reflecting on who God is and what He means to you (see Reflection 20). Rather than wanting something *from* Him, want *Him.*

PRAYER: Dear Lord, I admit that a lot of my prayer time is spent asking for stuff—regarding You only for what You can do for me instead of as the loving personal God that You are. May I begin to value our relationship together, not for what it can do for me, but what we mean to each other and how we can grow closer together. Thank You for my many blessings and for helping me to understand, with the help of the Holy Spirit, how loving You are. In Jesus' name, amen.

---

162 John Ortberg, *The Me I Want to Be: Becoming God's Best Version of You* (Grand Rapids: Zondervan, 2009), 245-248; Portions paraphrased.

92. A FRESH BLANKET OF SNOW

1 Corinthians 1:3. *Grace to you and peace from God our Father and the Lord Jesus Christ.*

Anthony Bloom has a wonderful analogy for how to start your day, which may provide a refreshing divergence from your difficult time.[163] Pretend that you are looking out on a fresh blanket of snow that does not have a footprint or a mark upon it. You have the opportunity to tread upon the snow however you like and make your unique mark upon it. One can't help but ask for God's blessing in such an endeavor because God created the beautiful, fresh, white blanket of snow upon which you will walk or run or skip or jump for joy or maybe make a snow angel. The vastness of the opportunity before you and the wide array of options that you have each morning is worthy of seeking God's blessing. Try to keep that image before you as the day unfolds—each step of the way is blessed by God and presents a fresh opportunity to walk as God's own messenger: to see God's hand in all that you do and with whomever you meet. Every circumstance you encounter is a gift of God, whether it is bitter or sweet, whether you like or dislike it. It is God's own gift to you, and, if you take it that way, then you can face any situation. God doesn't promise that everything will be rosy every day, but He does promise to be with you every step of your day and bless it.

PRAYER: Dear Lord, I do like to look out and see a blanket of virgin snow on the ground. There is a freshness, and everything is quieter and appears calmer. Thank You for creating that kind of an environment for me to start each day. Everything is fresh and new and awaiting Your blessing. It may not be the kind of day where everything goes my way, but it will be a day where You are walking with me and have blessed the outcome. In Jesus' name, amen.

---

163 Anthony Bloom, *Beginning to Pray* (New York: Paulist Press, 1970), 75.

93. THE GIFT OF UNCERTAINTY[164]

Luke 12:28. But if God so clothes the grass of the field, which is alive today and tomorrow is thrown into the oven, how much more will he clothe you— you of little faith!

You may not have thought of uncertainty as a gift, especially during your difficult time, but think of this: "it is uncertainty that demands that you get to know yourself really well—what you value, what you want— by questioning, choosing, risking and committing."[165] If we were certain about everything, including God, we wouldn't *need* faith and trust. As John Ortberg points out, "Trust is better than certainty because it honors the freedom of persons and makes possible growth and intimacy that certainty alone could never produce."[166] Rather than some vague trust in a concept, our trust is best placed in a person. Our faith is first and foremost a *relationship* with God, and what better way to live out that faith than by trusting the person of Jesus Christ. Ortberg gives an excellent example. What if you could put a camera on your spouse and know absolutely everything about him/her? It would give no room for uncertainty, but neither would it provide for any creativity or excitement in the relationship. Just like in the movie, *The Stepford Wives*, where the wives robotically did everything their husbands asked, your spouse would cease to relate to you in a meaningful, trusting way. When you trust, you take risks; you choose to be vulnerable; you give the gift of uncertainty. Meaningful relationships are built around trust: you trust someone for their recommendation of a good place to eat; you trust someone to keep confidential a secret you have told them; you trust that when you ask someone to go into partnership with you, that he won't "burn" you. You give a person the gift of your trust, and they, in return, give you the gift of their faithfulness. You don't have to force trust on someone; you don't accomplish it as an act of willpower; it develops over time. This is in large part why you can talk of faith as a gift: it grows out of knowing that you are trustworthy. When you are

---

164 John Ortberg, *Faith and Doubt* (Grand Rapids: Zondervan, 2008), 135-138; Portions paraphrased.
165 Ortberg, 136.
166 Ortberg, 137.

experiencing uncertainty in your difficult time, remember this reflection: uncertainty is a gift.

PRAYER: Dear Lord, Help me to see uncertainty as a gift. There are many times when I would rather be told exactly what to do by You, but, deep down, I realize that it would make me into a robot and cause me to lose my freedom, growth, and intimacy. My personal relationship with You is worth much to me, and I seek to grow in my relationship with You by taking risks—the risk to trust Your Word and live my life as Your faithful servant. In Jesus' name, amen.

94. ACTING ON YOUR PRAYERS[167]

Matthew 16:24. *Then Jesus told his disciples, "If any want to become my followers, let them deny themselves and take up their cross and follow me.*

When we ask for something of God, we must be prepared to act on it. We shouldn't ask to be relieved of a temptation, for example, when we are placing ourselves in a position to be tempted and relying on God to "bail us out." Prayer doesn't work like that. "When, in our prayers, we ask God to give us strength to do something in his name, we are not asking him to do it *instead* of us because we are too feeble to be willing to do it for ourselves."[168] God is willing to do His part if we are willing to do ours. At some point, we must take up our cross, knowing that we do not bear the burden alone (because Christ is at our side), but nevertheless knowing that we must do our part for God's kingdom on earth to be effective. We put all our talent and energy behind what we are praying for with all the power which God gives us. This is especially important in your difficult time. Your tendency may be to pray fervently and wait for God to act. Pray and act. Pray and act. You are not acting alone, but you are engaged; you are involved; you are acting on the promise that God is for you and with you and empowers you. If you are persistent and patient in this, your difficulties can't help but subside. However, it may take longer than you realize.

PRAYER: Dear Lord, Help me to pray and then act on what I pray about. I don't want to be like a person who just "sits on his heels" and expects God to do everything. I know that You act through me to further the interests of Your Kingdom. And, when everyone is acting on his prayers, powerful things happen. In Jesus' name, amen.

---

167 Anthony Bloom, *Beginning to Pray* (New York: Paulist Press, 1970), 55-64; Portions paraphrased.
168 Bloom, 64.

95. LISTENING FOR GOD[169]

1 Samuel 3:10. *Now the Lord came and stood there, calling as before, "Samuel! Samuel!" And Samuel said, "Speak, for your servant is listening."*

When in the midst of your difficult time, do you long to hear from God, or is that a normal part of your relationship with Him? Most people have developed the healthy habit of regularly talking to God and expressing themselves, but few claim to actually hear back from Him. But, why not? Jesus is your Friend (John 15:15), and friends talk to each other. Perhaps we are too limited in the manner in which we expect to hear from God. It isn't just the "still, small voice" inside us. It could be through a trusted friend or through something we read. God uses a variety of forms to communicate with us. And much as we want Him to be specific in what He tells us, God doesn't seem to work that way. He doesn't give us specific, step-by-step instructions any more than we would do so for our own children. There must be enough latitude to allow us to grow: God doesn't want us to be His robots, He wants us to fully utilize our creativity and energy to glorify His name. Be patient; listen; God will speak to you in His time and His way. Take comfort that the saints who preceded you heard from God—you can, too.

PRAYER: Dear Lord, It is easy to talk to You, but sometimes harder to discern what You are saying to me. Help me to develop the habit of listening for Your voice during my times of prayer and being attentive throughout the day for signs that You are speaking to me. I know that friendship implies two-way communication, and I seek to be more attentive to hearing from You. In Jesus' name, amen.

---

169 Dallas Willard, *Hearing God: Developing a Conversational Relationship with God* (Downers Grove: InterVarsity Press, 1984), 15-29; Portions paraphrased.

96. A SUFFERER'S PRAYER

Mark 14:36. [Jesus] said, "Abba, Father, for you all things are possible; re-move this cup from me; yet, not what I want, but what you want."

Here's a personal example of praying yourself through a difficult time. One night when I was trying to sleep I had difficulty breathing. My asthmatic bronchitis flared up due to an earlier infection. Despite all the medications from my doctor, I was still suffering and on top of that, was in a steroid induced high that had my mind racing. So, I prayed: "What are You trying to teach me, Lord? Is it to be humbler? Forgive my lack of humility, my arrogance, my tendency to think of myself as more important than I ought to. I repent. Is it my lack of character? Forgive my character flaws, my selfishness, my failure to relate to others. I repent. Is it my failure to trust You? Forgive my lack of trust, my ambitions that are driven by things outside Your will, my reliance on my own initiatives rather than prayerful consideration of how You are guiding me. I repent. Is it my failure to live in the moment? Forgive my anxiety, my constantly thinking about future events that are really in Your hands, my worry that my breathing will worsen rather than get better. Is it my lack of abandoning myself to You? Forgive me for selfish motives, for thinking of my own concerns first, for not relying on You. I repent. Is it my failure to intercede for others? Forgive my focus on myself rather than on so many others who are suffering worse trials than me. Help me to pray for them, and, in so doing, minimize my own preoccupation with my suffering. I repent." This is the prayer of a suffering Christian, a Christian going through a difficult time like you, and I thought that I would share it with you. Suffering is a "teachable moment." By the grace of God, the intensity of this prayer carried me to the point where I was due for my next breathing treatment, and I made it through the rest of the night with no further complications.

PRAYER: Dear Lord, I feel better now that I have prayed over my suffering. May my prayer resonate with others who are going through a difficult time and remind them that during times of suffering You are especially there, to teach us and comfort us. In Jesus' name, amen.

97. ANTICIPATING WHAT GOD WILL SAY

Matthew 8:8. The centurion answered, "Lord, I am not worthy to have you come under my roof; but only speak the word, and my servant will be healed."

Hearing from God is a subtle thing. Certainly, there is God's Word (the Bible) and the "still, small voice" (the Holy Spirit), but there is another aspect of "hearing" that goes beyond words. An analogy was brought to light most poignantly to me by Leslie Weatherhead:[170]

If my friend's mother in a distant town falls ill and he urgently desires to visit her, which would reveal deeper friendship—my lending him my motor-bike in response to his request for it, or my taking it to his door for him as soon as I heard of the need, without waiting to be asked? In the first case there has to be a request made with a voice. But in the second the fact of the friendship creates in me a longing to help. The first illustrates the communion between two persons on what we might call the level of the seen, but the second illustrates the communion, at a deeper level, of two persons on what we may call the level of the unseen.

While this example may not seem directly relevant to you in your difficult time, do you see the relevance to communicating with God? Mature Christians who have gotten to know how God works and are in personal relationship with Him *anticipate* His desires and directions without a specific command. We know it is "the right thing to do"—the thing that would please God. Please keep this in mind the next time you complain about not hearing anything from God: "In many cases our need to wonder about or be told what God wants in a certain situation is nothing short of a clear indication of how little we are engaged in his work."[171] In your difficult time, don't hold back from doing the things that will please God even before you consider praying about them. You know in advance that it is "the right thing to do" that will please God.

---

170 Dallas Willard, *Hearing God: Developing a Conversational Relationship with God* (Downers Grove: InterVarsity Press, 1984), 55; The author is quoting *The Transforming Friendship* by Leslie Weatherhead.
171 Willard, 55.

PRAYER: Dear Lord, Wow! I never thought of it that way. When I seek first Your Kingdom and its righteousness, I am developing a way of communicating with You that transcends the need for words (Matthew 6:33)! I learn to recognize what pleases You and "just do it." Help me to be so engaged in Your work that this becomes natural for me. In Jesus' name, amen.

98. THE COST OF LOOKING FOR SOMETHING MORE[172]

Matthew 24:21. *For at that time there will be great suffering, such as has not been from the beginning of the world until now, no, and never will be.*

Are you disillusioned with life? Are things not going your way? It's tough to reconcile, but God is in your life. Consider these consoling words from Richard Rohr: "Normally the way God pushes us is by disillusioning us with the present mode. Until the present falls apart, we will never look for Something More. We will never discover what it is that really sustains us. But that dreaded experience is always suffering in some form. . . . [Suffering] seems to be the price of the death of the small self and the emergence of the True Self, when we finally come to terms with our true identity in God."[173] Yes, it is hard to go through difficult times and suffer. Consider it the cost of looking for Something More. Isn't there another way? Apparently not, or God would have thought of it. Christ suffered and transformed the world. We suffer in order to be transformed into His image. It is as simple (and as difficult) as that. Suffering is a fact of life and allows us to find our True Self in Christ.

PRAYER: Dear Lord, I don't want to suffer. But, it is Your way. It is the path to transformation. Help me to have Your perspective and to be willing to suffer in order to be transformed into Your image. As a child of God, I have much to learn, and, like it or not, some of that learning happens in the crucible of suffering. In Jesus' name, amen.

---

172 Richard Rohr, *Hope Against Darkness: The Transforming Vision of Saint Francis in an Age of Anxiety* (Cincinnati: St. Anthony Messenger Press, 2001), 1070-1090; Portions paraphrased.

173 Rohr, 1080.

99. REVERSE YOUR STRUGGLE

Ephesians 2:8-9. *For by grace you have been saved through faith, and this is not your own doing; it is the gift of God— not the result of works, so that no one may boast.*

Sometimes we get the order of doing things backwards, and this is true in our relationship to God. We think that we must do things right in order to have God love us and in order to come to believe in God. Instead, it is our belief in God (which is His gift to us) which leads us to do the right things. This was a difficult lesson for me to learn. I was constantly "working" at my faith, as if it were something I had to earn before I could move into a closer relationship with God. I still remember vividly the moment I came to realize that I had things backwards. I was at a Bible study on Ephesians where we had just read the wonderful verses Ephesians 2:8-9, "For by grace you have been saved through faith, and this is not your own doing; it is the gift of God— not the result of works, so that no one may boast." I walked out of that class floating on air, because I no longer had to work at my faith but could receive it and marvel at it and let it flow into me and govern my life—with no struggle on my part! So, the next time you think that your faith is faltering, pause and reverse your struggle—first comes the gift of faith, then comes your loving and obedient response. Once you grasp this concept, start acting on it. As Richard Rohr says, "You cannot think yourself into a new way of living, but you must live yourself into a new way of thinking."[174] Live in this manner, with things in the proper sequence, and see if it doesn't help you through your difficult time.

PRAYER: Dear Lord, It has been a struggle to be obedient to You. Maybe I'm trying too hard on my own. First comes the faith, Your gift to us, and then obedience and love can flow. Thank You for this insight. In Jesus' name, amen.

---

174 Richard Rohr, *Hope Against Darkness: The Transforming Vision of Saint Francis in an Age of Anxiety* (Cincinnati: St. Anthony Messenger Press, 2001), 948.

100. SAYING "YES" TO GOD AND "NO" TO THE LIES OF THIS WORLD[175]

Matthew 3:2. *Repent, for the kingdom of heaven has come near.*

There comes a time in a man's heart when he realizes that there is more to life than what he sees; more to life than the ways of this world. His eyes are turned to spiritual matters, and he decides to change his ways and priorities. This decision to change from the world's way to God's way is called repentance. We disavow our allegiance to political systems, commercialism, materialism, striving for more money, and recognize it for what it is: a futile attempt to convince us that man, in his own power, can make things right. We repent, we change, we turn to God. "It is the turning point marking the transition from a dreaming nostalgia for a better life to a rugged pilgrimage of discipleship in faith, from complaining about your difficult time to pursuing all things good."[176] Not that things instantly get better. But, now we have hope. God has a plan for our lives. God is in control of the cosmos and has declared it good. In Jesus Christ, we have a Savior and a suffering Servant and Lord and Master who understands our plight and who has preceded us in suffering—the ultimate suffering that has removed our sins from us as far as East is from West (Psalm 103:12). Eugene Peterson says that repentance is a powerful decision that says "yes" to God and "no" to the lies of this world. It is a fundamental and important step forward in a person's faith journey. You are having a difficult time. If it is because you are dependent on the ways of this world, repent! Turn to God, say a prayer, rest in His gracious provision for your life and His ultimate promise of a complete life with Him.

PRAYER: Dear Lord, I repent. I have decided to say "yes" to you and "no" to the ways of this world. I realize that I am still in the world, and life will continue to provide challenges and disappointments, but now I have Your perspective on things, which provides a source of joy and comfort no matter what my circumstances. In Jesus' name, amen.

---

175 Eugene H. Peterson, *A Long Obedience in the Same Direction: Discipleship in an Instant Society* (Downers Grove: InterVarsity Press, 1980), 21-25; Portions paraphrased.

176 Peterson, 24.

101. GOD REFUSES TO BE ABSTRACT[177]

Job 42:1-2. Then Job answered the LORD: "I know that you can do all things, and that no purpose of yours can be thwarted."

What lesson did Job learn as a result of his suffering? One important thing was that he could be in dialogue with his God about his dilemma and trust that God is in control (See Job 42). Before his suffering, he was not nearly as attuned to God. Afterwards, he knows that God takes him seriously and he is "in the conversation." And, what a conversation it is! God reveals His magnificence and creativity and restores Job to a life of prosperity and blessing. Job learned that God can be trusted—that the world is after all a place of blessing and safety and coherence. "We do not really need answers (Job never really got an answer); we only need to be taken seriously as part of the dialogue. But we only know this in hindsight after the suffering and the struggle. It cannot be known theoretically or theologically or before the fact."[178] God refuses to be an abstract thought—He wants to enter into our situation and be relevant through the passion and pain of it all. That means we must be willing to face the darkness in faith that we will learn from it and be in more intimate dialogue with our God as a result. Hopefully, this puts your difficult time into a proper perspective—God is getting your attention. He is becoming more and more relevant and real to you.

PRAYER: Dear Lord, Why we must suffer is one of the great mysteries of life. But if it makes You more relevant and real to us, it is worth it. After our suffering, we are in more intimate dialogue with You; we understand how things work together for good; we develop a stronger bond and level of trust with You. Thank You for caring enough about us to help us to go through suffering and be drawn closer to You. In Jesus' name, amen.

---

177 Richard Rohr, *Hope Against Darkness: The Transforming Vision of Saint Francis in an Age of Anxiety* (Cincinnati: St. Anthony Messenger Press, 2001), 1590-1595; Portions paraphrased.
178 Rohr, 1595.

102. GOD'S UNFAILING PROTECTION AND READINESS TO FORGIVE

Matthew 26:28. *For this is my blood of the covenant, which is poured out for many for the forgiveness of sins.*

"Our security is no longer based on anything we might possess or accomplish, but rather on our conviction of God's unfailing protection and readiness to forgive."[179] It has taken me a long time to grasp the significance of this statement by Thomas Keating, and, even then, I can take it in for only fleeting moments before my mind takes over, and I once again seek security in worldly things. Wouldn't it be wonderful if our sole security were based on "God's unfailing protection and readiness to forgive?" The contemplative lifestyle is based on this premise. It accommodates this darkness, this paradox of being anxious and even fearful of our worldly security, while at the same time living in the light of God's promises. Richard Rohr advises, "We must not get rid of the anxiety until we have learned what it wants to teach us."[180] Rohr elaborates that we must resist the temptation to quickly solve problems, even though we all like to be models of efficiency and productivity. When we stop trying to control every situation, we begin to realize that there is Someone Else in control of the Big Picture, and we allow ourselves to be part of the flow of life and our anxiety subsides. This "letting go" doesn't happen overnight; it doesn't even happen that often, and it may take a while during your difficult time, but, when it does, it will carry you over until the next time. It often gets a foothold during our times of quiet before God.

PRAYER: Dear Lord, Help me to be silent before You and to bask in the magnificence of Your creation, and grasp that, while You love me, and I am important, there is more to life than just me. I want to be part of this "flow of life" and reduce my anxiety over my difficult time—but not too quickly, for my problems have much to teach me. In Jesus' name, amen.

---

179 Thomas Keating, *The Daily Reader for Contemplative Living: Excerpts from the Works of Father Thomas Keating* (New York: Continuum, 2006), 194.
180 Richard Rohr, *Everything Belongs: The Gift of Contemplative Prayer* (New York: Crossroad, 2003), 144.

103. ON TEMPTATION[181]

1 Corinthians 10:13. *No testing has overtaken you that is not common to everyone. God is faithful, and he will not let you be tested beyond your strength, but with the testing he will also provide the way out so that you may be able to endure it.*

"We become vulnerable to temptation when we are dissatisfied with our lives."[182] Since you are going through a difficult time, you are likely dissatisfied with some aspect of your life. Therefore, you must be particularly on guard for temptation. John Ortberg points out that we were made for "soul satisfaction." If we don't find it in God, we seek it elsewhere. And looking elsewhere takes us right into temptation. If we seek to repress temptation and desire on our own, it will wear us out. We need an advocate, and, fortunately, we have one in the Holy Spirit. We can be free with the help of the Spirit to choose not to submit to temptation; not to be enslaved by our appetites. As Ortberg states, "Real freedom is not the external freedom to gratify every appetite; it is the internal freedom not to be enslaved by our appetites, to have a place to stand so that we are not mastered by them."[183] And the place to stand is in the community of faith. It is hard, if not impossible, to resist temptation on our own. But, fortunately, we have fellow Christians with whom we can receive support, advice, and comfort. Maybe you don't share your deepest temptations with everyone, but you are blessed indeed if you have one or two friends with whom you can confide everything and know that it will be kept in confidence. As the apostle Paul says, "No testing has overtaken you that is not common to everyone. God is faithful, and he will not let you be tested beyond your strength, but with the testing he will also provide the way out so that you may be able to endure it" (1 Corinthians 10:13). The best "way out" is through a friend. Remember, everyone faces temptation. In fact, temptation may very well come to us where we need most to grow: if it's patience, we will meet some trying people; if it's envy, there will be someone

---

181 John Ortberg, *The Me I Want to Be: Becoming God's Best Version of You* (Grand Rapids: Zondervan, 2009), 140-143; Portions paraphrased.
182 Ortberg, 141.
183 Ortberg, 140.

or something desirous placed in front of you; if it's greed, money matters may consume you. But with God's help, you can turn from temptation to the wonderful avenues of soul satisfaction that your faith provides.

PRAYER: Dear Lord, Help me to stand up under temptation with Your help. I am hungry for "soul satisfaction," but I know that it is not found in the ways of this world, but rather in the ways of Your Kingdom. Right now, I am going through a difficult time, and I feel particularly vulnerable to temptation. It will likely come in areas where I need to grow. I stand firm with the apostle Paul in knowing that God will not let me be tempted beyond what I can bear. Thank You for my friends in Christ who will help me confront and conquer my temptations. In Jesus' name, amen.

104. KEYS TO A WISE AND MORAL LIFE

Acts 15:12. *The whole assembly kept silence, and listened to Barnabas and Paul as they told of all the signs and wonders that God had done through them among the Gentiles.*

Here are the traits that Richard Rohr says are key to being wise and living a moral life: silence, solitude, detachment, honesty, confession, forgiveness, and radical humility.[184] Do they resonate with you? They are listed by a Franciscan monk, so perhaps they have more of a contemplative flavor than you are accustomed, to, but they are worth practicing. I have touched on all of them in earlier reflections and will continue to do so throughout this book. Silence and solitude are sometimes hard to come by in this rapid-paced world we live in. Try to "get away from it all" by carving out a specific time to read these reflections and meditate. Detachment means that we aren't snared by the consumerism, power, and sex frenzy of this world. Honesty needs no further explanation. It is hard to be at peace with yourself if you are being deceitful. Confession is a hallmark of the Christian life—a confessed life is a redeemed life. Forgiveness is another cornerstone of Christianity—"forgive us our debts, as we forgive our debtors" (Matthew 6:12). Radical humility means that we aren't pretending to be humble, but truly have a servant-attitude toward our fellow man. Take these traits to heart and you will not be disappointed. They are best learned by the practice of *living*, especially in the midst of your difficult time.

PRAYER: Dear Lord, Help me to practice the disciplines of silence, solitude, detachment, honesty, confession, forgiveness, and radical humility. By doing so, I become wiser and closer to you. I need to take time out of my busy schedule to be attentive to these disciplines. I can't do them on my own, but, with Your help, I can draw closer and closer to modeling the ways that You consider important to growing in faith and wisdom. In Jesus' name, amen.

---

184 Richard Rohr, *Hope Against Darkness: The Transforming Vision of Saint Francis in an Age of Anxiety* (Cincinnati: St. Anthony Messenger Press, 2001), 1581.

105. BEARING THE MYSTERY[185]

Romans 15:31b-32. *[I, Paul, pray] that my ministry to Jerusalem may be acceptable to the saints, so that by God's will I may come to you with joy and be refreshed in your company.*

How we long for certainty in this life! To have everything laid out for us and know the direction we should go. But God doesn't operate like that. Who of us can say for certain that we are doing God's will? Even the great contemplative Thomas Merton at the end of his life said, "I don't know if I've ever done your will, all I know is that I want to do your will. I'm not certain that I'm pleasing you. All I know is that I want to please you."[186] That's part of the mystery of God. Not knowing for sure. But He does give us lots of hints as to what pleases Him, and a lot of latitude within those hints. Thank God for that! It wouldn't turn out well to have everything spelled out for us. Likewise, we can't put God in a box and have Him all figured out and know exactly what pleases Him; how to do His will perfectly. Yes, it's sometimes very unsatisfying not to know whether you are doing God's will, especially when you are going through a difficult time. As Richard Rohr says, "That's what it means to 'bear the mystery,' to hang with Jesus on the horns of the human dilemma, to agree to find God in a clearly imperfect world."[187] God loves us, warts and all. He knows that we are imperfect and can't hope to be in His will all the time. But that's OK. It's part of the mystery. Part of the beauty of life.

PRAYER: Dear Lord, I can't tell whether I'm doing Your will for my life. All I know is that I want to. But it's comforting to know that You love me even when I fall short. Help me to "bear the mystery" and hang in there with You. I don't need to be perfect to be loved, and that is a source of comfort. In Jesus' name, amen.

---

185 Richard Rohr, *Hope Against Darkness: The Transforming Vision of Saint Francis in an Age of Anxiety* (Cincinnati: St. Anthony Messenger Press, 2001), 717-718; Paraphrased.

186 Rohr, 717.

187 Rohr, 720.

106. HOW TO CATCH A BUTTERFLY

Romans 8:25. *But if we hope for what we do not see, we wait for it with patience.*

I read an interesting metaphor for patience the other day. To catch a butterfly, don't run around after them flailing your arms and hoping to snag one. Instead, sit patiently and eventually one will land on your shoulder. That is how our approach to God should be. We spend a lot of energy "flailing around" after God. Thinking that if we try a little harder, work at it more, we will somehow capture God: fully understand Him, have Him in our pocket; know what He is all about and overcome our difficult time. Instead, God finds us: the butterfly lands on our shoulder. We are enlightened through no major effort on our part. That does not mean that there is NO effort on our part. We are to seek first the Kingdom and its righteousness, but not with the objective of figuring God out—He is far too grand and mysterious for that (Matthew 6:33). Be content to have God find you. It is often in the "little things" of life—enjoying nature or spending time with our friends—that we become most aware.

PRAYER: Dear Lord, Give me patience to let the butterfly land on my shoulder. I spend a lot of wasted energy in pursuing You on my own, as if I can capture You. You are too grand and mysterious for that. Let me be content that You find me in Your way; often in the "little things" of life. In Jesus' name, amen.

107. THE CRUCIFORM PATTERN OF LIFE[188]

Romans 9:33. *See, I am laying in Zion a stone that will make people stumble, a rock that will make them fall, and whoever believes in him will not be put to shame.*

There is a cruciform pattern to life that Richard Rohr likens to taking three steps forward and two steps backward in our faith journey. None of us likes the two steps backward part. It is a loss, a feeling of futility, a feeling that God is not on your side; that He doesn't care. The church is going through a two steps backwards phase of its life: losing members, losing perceived relevance; struggling to be heard. "Yet Jesus shows us on the cross that this is the only and constant pattern, and we should not be shocked or surprised by it."[189] We are a people who live in contradictions, who must learn to cope with the complexities of life yet still be true to our faith. We are the faithful remnant that keeps the world from spinning out of control. We are the agents of all true transformation, reconciliation, and newness.

PRAYER: Dear Lord, It's painful to take two steps backward. But such is the mystery of Your suffering servanthood. Not all is rosy or movement forward. I certainly realize that in my difficult time. But, there is meaning and purpose in the backward journey. It is a necessary part of transformation. Jesus went through it on the cross; we go through it in real life. But it is a renewing process; a necessary step in our faith journey that allows growth. Help me to accept this aspect of my faith and my difficult time. In Jesus' name, amen.

---

188 Richard Rohr, *Hope Against Darkness: The Transforming Vision of Saint Francis in an Age of Anxiety* (Cincinnati: St. Anthony Messenger Press, 2001), 690-700; Portions paraphrased.
189 Rohr, 697.

108. DEVELOPING A CALM MIND

Luke 8:24. *They went to him and woke him up, shouting, "Master, Master, we are perishing!" And he woke up and rebuked the wind and the raging waves; they ceased, and there was a calm.*

Toward the end of my career as a Project Manager for a large manufacturing firm, I was put in charge of a project that, while important, had long periods of relative inactivity during which I was at wits' ends. I remember sitting at my desk trying to keep myself "busy." I would check my email, go over my project plan, see if I had any phone messages, and then repeat the process over and over. What a waste! The worst part was the feeling that I *had* to be busy. That was the corporate mantra: busyness at all costs. Now that I've retired, I still have periods of relative inactivity, but I find them calming rather than disturbing. I think, in large measure, my meditation has helped calm and concentrate my mind. There is nothing worse than a monkey-like mind that is wandering all over the place and can't concentrate under the guise of "multitasking." There are exercises that will help you develop a calm mind. See, for example, the wonderful exercises in the book *Essential Spirituality* by Roger Walsh, especially the chapter, "Practice Four: Concentrate and Calm Your Mind" (147-171). "A calm mind offers a clear mirror with which to look out at the world and in at ourselves."[190] It's like a lake, which is most lucid when the water is still, like a mirror. If part of your difficult time is over this struggle to be "busy," where your mind is all over the place, develop a practice of calming the mind.

PRAYER: Dear Lord, I have fallen victim to the need to feel "busy" and "productive" all the time, and my mind is all over the place. Help me to concentrate and focus on the moment in a calm manner in order to appreciate life rather than rush through it. My time of prayer is a calming moment, as is my time to read these reflections and consider them. Thank You for being the source of calm in my life. In Jesus' name, amen.

---

190 Roger Walsh, *Essential Spirituality: The 7 Central Practices to Awaken Heart and Mind* (New York: John Wiley and Sons, 1999), 171.

109. GOD'S UNCONDITIONAL LOVE[191]

John 13:34. *I give you a new commandment, that you love one another. Just as I have loved you, you also should love one another.*

God is love. And Jesus Christ is the embodiment of that love. "God's love was revealed among us in this way: God sent His only Son into the world so that we might live through Him. In this is love, not that we loved God but that He loved us and sent His Son to be the atoning sacrifice for our sins" (1 John 4:9-10). God's love is unconditional: there are no strings attached. There is nothing we can do to make God love us anymore, and nothing we can do to make God love us any less. He loves us. Period. We are so accustomed to having to be a winner or striving to do our best in our work life or in sports or in our relationships, that we forget that, in Jesus Christ, you do not have to be good enough, to perform, to be a winner. In fact, as Patrick Morley points out, "Ironically to be in Christ means exactly the opposite—it is to admit that you are not good enough, that you cannot perform, that because of sin's grip on your life you are a loser—and to admit, for that very reason, that you need a Savior, a Savior whose unconditional love transforms your life."[192] This idea should be a comfort to you in your difficult times. Can you love in this way? Once you do, you will find that others will love you the same way. Not because you sought them out, but because of the example you have set. They want to reciprocate what they experience in you. Loving in this way—unconditionally and in Christ—is a wonderful way to release yourself from your problems and worries: as a child of God you are loved no matter what your circumstances.

PRAYER: Dear Lord, Thank You for loving me unconditionally and taking the pressure off me to be a "success" in the eyes of this world. You love me for who I am, not for what I can or cannot do, and despite my problems and shortcomings. And, when I follow Your example and love others this way, You are pleased, and, in return, I am loved by others in the same manner. In Jesus' name, amen.

---

191 Patrick Morley, *Ten Secrets for the Man in the Mirror* (Grand Rapids: Zondervan, 2000), 157-158.
192 Morley, 157.

110. A LIFE OF SIMPLICITY[193]

Galatians 5:22. *The fruit of the Spirit is love, joy, peace, patience, kindness, generosity, faithfulness, gentleness, and self-control. There is no law against such things.*

It's hard working within "the system." There are a lot of demands of modern society that create a lot of stress and "churn" without much payoff. At least, not the kind of payoff that is important. Jesus faced a lot of societal demands—demands that He conform to the norms of His day and "toe the line." What did He do? "He preached a life of simplicity outside the system of power, money and control. He built an alternative worldview where power, prestige and possessions were not sought or even admired."[194] His alternate lifestyle of simplicity is one that we can embrace today. Societal rules have no power over us because we have different priorities. For example, we are not tempted to cheat on our tax returns, because they can be done in a straightforward manner without all the accoutrements of fancy tax write-offs. Remember the "fruit of the spirit" (Galatians 5:22, above) against which there is no law. A life of simplicity modeled after Jesus has much to be said for it. Your loyalties revolve around obedience to God rather than obedience to "the system." You are not obsessed with getting more money, climbing the corporate ladder, earning that next big promotion, getting the corner office as much as you are with loving your neighbor as yourself and your God above all else. In your difficult time, try to simplify things—and do what Jesus would do.

PRAYER: Dear Lord, A life of simplicity has much to be said for it. Rather than join the corporate "rat race," I can embrace what the fruit of the Spirit has to offer and follow the example of Jesus. He was not beholden to societal norms when they went against His principles, and I don't need to be either. In Jesus' name, amen.

---

193 Richard Rohr, *Hope Against Darkness: The Transforming Vision of Saint Francis in an Age of Anxiety* (Cincinnati: St. Anthony Messenger Press, 2001), 950-960.
194 Rohr, 955.

III. KNOWN BY OUR FRUITS[195]

Matthew 7:16. *You will know them by their fruits. Are grapes gathered from thorns, or figs from thistles?*

Our very craving for God shows us that God is present, although in a hidden way, in our lives. Look at Mother Teresa. After her death, her memoirs showed that she suffered a great deal over her own personal doubts about the existence of God. And yet, she healed so many in His name, and she ministered as though everyone she treated were the face of Jesus Himself. How wonderfully redemptive! Jesus said, "you will know them by their fruits" (Matthew 7:16). Not by their certainty you shall know them—by their fruits. Press on! There is a world of good we can do out there rather than wallowing in our uncertainty and doubt and concern over our difficult time. John Ortberg says, "We cannot see God as he is. We are not capable of this. We inevitably project our own fallenness onto God. God seems to present himself to us in such a way that people who want to dismiss God will be able to dismiss him."[196] Sure, we would like more objective evidence of the existence of God. But God has chosen to let us struggle with the realities of life while He seems to be silent. There is much to be said for the freedoms we enjoy. We would not like it if God were so invasive in our lives that we felt like robots, doing His commands because He dictated that they be carried out in a certain way. So, uncertainty has its benefits in the freedom it provides. Unfortunately, we often abuse those freedoms, and others outside the faith have a hard time seeing God in our actions. One person described Christians as "very conservative, entrenched in their thinking, anti-gay, anti-choice, angry, violent, illogical, empire builders, they want to convert everyone, and they generally cannot live peacefully with anyone who doesn't believe what they believe."[197] Wow! I hope that we don't all resemble that stereotype. It is troubling that some people see us that way. We must be on our guard to be more loving and humble and Christ-like and to repent when we fall short. The freedoms we

---

195 John Ortberg, *Faith and Doubt* (Grand Rapids: Zondervan, 2008), 110-112; Portions paraphrased.
196 Ortberg, 110.
197 Ortberg, 112.

enjoy as Christians must not result in letting people stereotype us in rigid, unloving ways. As you go through your difficult time, be grateful for the freedoms you enjoy, and let people know you by your fruits.

PRAYER: Dear Lord, I am a fallen, broken person, and yet I know that You love me. Let me use my freedom to further Your cause and to think beyond my personal difficulties, so that people know me by my fruits. May they be pleasing to You. In Jesus' name, amen.

112. DRAWING CLOSER TO GOD[198]

Luke 6:12. *Now during those days he went out to the mountain to pray; and he spent the night in prayer to God.*

I have talked about the importance of having a time and a place to pray (See Reflection 1). If you can't always be in your place of prayer, consider taking a special symbol of God's love; a cross or an icon, to remind you of His presence. And if you can't honor the time you have arranged to pray, consider praying during the transitions of your day: when you get up, when you eat breakfast, when you drive to work, before a meeting, before lunch, on the drive home, when you pick up the kids at one of their events, before dinner, when you go to bed—any time that you undergo change. Times of change are a time of particular vulnerability when closeness to God is especially important. If your workplace does not condone the practice of prayer before meetings (most don't), consider starting each meeting with a time of silence, where the people that are present can set aside the concerns and issues that are not germane to the task at hand. These are some small but important ways that you can draw closer to God during your day so that you are helped through your difficult time.

PRAYER: Dear Lord, I recognize that the transition points in my day are times of particular vulnerability. No one likes times of change, and it is helpful to invoke Your presence during them. I can't always be at my designated place and time for prayer, and these suggestions for how to draw close to You during the day are helpful. Thank You for the opportunity to pray at any time of day or night. In Jesus' name, amen.

---

198 Gregory F. Augustine Pierce, *Spirituality at Work: 10 Ways to Balance Your Life on the Job* (Chicago: Loyola Press, 2005), Kindle, 402-502; Portions paraphrased.

113. WORSHIP IS A DECREE FROM GOD

Psalm 100:4. *Enter his gates with thanksgiving, and his courts with praise. Give thanks to him, bless his name.*

Are you still having difficulty making it to your worship service every Sunday? True, it is voluntary. Despite the recent decline in church attendance, it is still the most important thing that Christians can do. So, what is holding you back? Eugene Peterson says that maybe it would help if you thought of worship as a decree from God. Psalm 122 talks about the pilgrimage of the Israelites to Jerusalem and says "[it was] *decreed* for Israel, to give thanks to the name of the Lord" (Psalm 122:4). And, their way of giving thanks was to worship. Even if you don't feel like going to worship, perhaps because of your difficult time, you should do it anyway. As Eugene Peterson points out, "the wisdom of God says . . .that we can *act* ourselves into a new way of feeling much quicker than we can *feel* ourselves into a new way of acting. Worship is an act which develops feelings for God, not a feeling for God which is expressed in an act of worship."[199] Do you see what he is saying? I wish I had a dime for every time my family members said, "But I don't feel like going to church." I'd be a rich man. But, once you have a mindset that worship is a decree from God and is independent of your feelings of the moment, you will be more prone to go to church. Act on the decree. Go to worship. Then, at the conclusion of worship, you will undoubtedly feel better that you went.

PRAYER: Dear Lord, Help me to be more diligent in my worship attendance. Now I know that I can take action to go to worship without relying on my feelings. I can act myself into worship, and, in the resulting time of praise and thanksgiving, be glad that I went. In Jesus' name, amen.

---

199 Eugene H. Peterson, *A Long Obedience in the Same Direction: Discipleship in an Instant Society* (Downers Grove: InterVarsity Press, 1980), 50.

114. SUFFERING AND DEATH ARE PART OF GOD'S CREATION[200]

Matthew 4:16. *The people who sat in darkness have seen a great light, and for those who sat in the region and shadow of death light has dawned.*

Here is Ilia Delio's perspective on death and suffering. She says, "If we could only realize that suffering and death are part of God's creation, we would accept them, for we desire to become a new creation. If we knew that pain and suffering touch the heart of God, we would allow them to touch us as well, for what we seek is God's heart of love."[201] God suffers along with us. Suffering and death are part of His plan. We can't understand that completely, but all we need to do is look around and see that suffering and death are indeed surrounding us and very much part and parcel of the conduct of the universe. What Delio is proposing is that we embrace suffering and death in recognition that they are part of the process of becoming a new creation—God helps us to evolve into new creatures that are more closely identified with Him via the route of pain, suffering, and, yes, even death. "God loves those who suffer, shares their pain, and bears their burdens with them."[202] May we be so bold as to accept the role of suffering in our lives—no, not only accept, but embrace it.

PRAYER: Dear Lord, No one wants to suffer, and yet we see it all around us. It is so prevalent that it must be part of God's plan for us. Help me to accept my times of suffering and to sense Your presence and the unfolding of the cosmos within its grasp. In Jesus' name, amen.

---

200 Ilia Delio, *The Humility of God: A Franciscan Perspective* (Cincinnati: St. Anthony Messenger Press, 2011), 1645-1655; Portions paraphrased.
201 Delio, 1647.
202 Delio, 1755.

115. PATHWAYS TO GOD

Psalm 16:11. *You show me the path of life. In your presence there is fullness of joy; in your right hand are pleasures forevermore.*

There is no "one size fits all" set of spiritual disciplines. God made each of us unique; therefore, our approach to God must be unique. Certainly, reading and understanding Scripture is our primary path to knowing God. But, there are other "spiritual disciplines" that can augment and help to complete your time with the Bible. Perhaps, you are inspired by a walk in nature or singing hymns at the worship service. Some of the pathways that John Ortberg points out are:[203]

Naturalist	Finds God in nature
Ascetic	Is drawn to disciplines
Traditionalist	Loves historical liturgies
Activist	Comes alive spiritually in a great cause
Caregiver	Meets God in serving
Sensate	Senses God through the five senses
Enthusiast	Loves to grow through people
Contemplative	Is drawn to solitary reflection and prayer
Intellectual	Loves God by learning

You just have to try out what comes naturally and "feels right." Take time out from the difficult time you are having and find one or two disciplines that will work for you to augment your time with the Bible.

---

203 John Ortberg, *The Me I Want to Be: Becoming God's Best Version of You* (Grand Rapids: Zondervan, 2009), 55.

PRAYER: Dear Lord, Thank You for creating us all uniquely. Help me to find the set of spiritual disciplines that draws me closest to You. When I find them, help me to use them regularly and frequently to draw close to You. It is through the exercise of spiritual disciplines that I can grow in my faith and put my problems in perspective. In Jesus' name, amen.

116. THE BENEFITS OF SERVICE[204]

2 Corinthians 9:11. *You will be enriched in every way for your great generosity, which will produce thanksgiving to God through us.*

Here is an important key to overcoming your difficulties. Live a life of service to others and be willing to share your possessions. "Our service to others serves us in several ways: It weakens negative forces and strengthens positive ones within our minds. When we share our possessions, time, or energy, we loosen the heavy chains of greed, jealousy, and fear of loss that bind us to our egos. Likewise, when emotions such as love and happiness are expressed as kindness, they grow stronger in the process."[205] We become that which we give away: if we desire happiness for others, thoughts of happiness first fill our own minds and overflow into caring actions. Our motives for giving are key. If we expect something in return, it is not altruistic giving. It is a form of manipulation—giving in order to get what we want from the other person. There is a strong spiritual component to service, and we don't need to wait until we are "enlightened" to serve. "The best way to become a better helper is to become a better person. But one necessary aspect of becoming a better person is via helping other people. So one must and can do both simultaneously."[206] So, start your acts of generosity now, and, through them, become a better person.

PRAYER: Dear Lord, I know that Your life was one of service. Help me to model mine after Yours. Although I needn't expect any return from my giving and service, I understand that there are untold benefits to my spirituality and happiness when I open up and serve. Show me the way and the need, and I will serve. In Jesus' name, amen.

---

204 Roger Walsh, *Essential Spirituality: The 7 Central Practices to Awaken Heart and Mind* (New York: John Wiley and Sons, 1999), 255-258; Portions paraphrased.
205 Walsh, 255.
206 Walsh, 258; Quoting Abraham Maslow.

117. HOW TO CULTIVATE A GENEROUS HEART[207]

1 Samuel 20:4. *Then Jonathan said to David, "Whatever you say, I will do for you."*

Yesterday, we talked about the benefits of service. Today, we will cover how to cultivate a generous heart. Certainly, one way is to expose yourself to others who have learned the gift of humble service—it rubs off. Secondly, find a way to serve by doing something that you like to do. Service doesn't have to equate to drudgery—in fact, often what you like to do is also what makes the best use of your talents. Third, doublecheck your motivation to serve. It should not be done with a sense of obligation, tension, or annoyance. First, explore those feelings and even say no to requests for service until you can do them with openheartedness and genuine caring. Fourth, start small. Get used to the good feeling that comes from giving, and then slowly increase it as you get comfortable with service. Mother Teresa urged, "Don't look for spectacular actions. What is important is the gift of yourselves. It is the degree of love you insert in your deeds [that is important]."[208] I hope that these tips help you to overcome your difficulties by embracing and growing a life of service.

PRAYER: Dear Lord, I will seek ways to serve that make the best use of my time and talents. Help me to serve with a sense of openheartedness and genuine caring. I don't need to do something spectacular but something that is pleasing to You. In Jesus' name, amen.

---

207 Roger Walsh, *Essential Spirituality: The 7 Central Practices to Awaken Heart and Mind* (New York: John Wiley and Sons, 1999), 262-265; Portions paraphrased.
208 Walsh, 263.

118. AWAKENING SERVICE

Acts 26:16. But get up and stand on your feet; for I have appeared to you for this purpose, to appoint you to serve and testify to the things in which you have seen me and to those in which I will appear to you.

Roger Walsh uses the term "awakening service" to describe service that is done with three goals in mind.[209] First, dedicate your service to a higher goal. See it as a way to develop increased awareness and a more refined level of wisdom. The higher goal may be for the good of one's family or the welfare of the world or to fulfill God's will for your life. Going above and beyond the personal reasons for your service is more rewarding in the long haul. Second, relinquish attachments to specific outcomes. We touched on this earlier in the previous two reflections. If things work out differently from what we expect, or, if we are not lavished with praise, our attachments go unfulfilled and we suffer accordingly. Learn from your service, don't be governed by the outcome. Lastly, learn from your experience. Instead of being governed by the outcome, be surprised at the outcome, and learn from it. If it wasn't what you expected, instead of getting upset, see what the outcome is teaching you and grow from it. "Through awakening service we simultaneously purify motivation, weaken cravings, serve as best we can, and learn how to serve and awaken more effectively in the future."[210] Just what we need to deal with our difficult time.

PRAYER: Dear Lord, Service is a mutually rewarding experience. When I do it for You, I am reminded of how You served when You were among us, and I am pleased to follow Your example. When I do it without expectation of what I think the outcome should be, I grow. When I remain open to however the service plays out, I learn from it. Help me to be an effective servant. In Jesus' name, amen.

---

209 Roger Walsh, *Essential Spirituality: The 7 Central Practices to Awaken Heart and Mind* (New York: John Wiley and Sons, 1999), 264.
210 Walsh, 266.

119. LIVE LIFE TO THE FULLEST

Richard Rohr. *The edges of our lives—fully experienced, suffered and enjoyed—lead us back to the center and the essence.*

Throughout these reflections, I have been a strong advocate of prayer and meditation. But Richard Rohr points out an even better way of finding our deepest and most profound selves: by living life to the fullest. That's why I've spent so much time emphasizing the importance of living fully in the present moment. We find what is already there—the unfathomable love of God and the mystery of the cosmos, by living and fully accepting our reality. "Living and accepting our reality will not feel very spiritual. It will feel like we are on the edges rather than dealing with the essence. But the edges of our lives—fully experienced, suffered and enjoyed—lead us back to the center and the essence."[211] Rohr says it's a matter of bearing the mystery of God's suffering and joy inside ourselves. Yes, you are going through a difficult time—suffering in some way. But, your suffering leads to spiritual enlightenment and fulfillment. No, it doesn't feel like it now, but when you acknowledge the suffering as part of God's plan—unexplainable as it is—you begin the process of becoming whole and complete. So, living life to its fullest—suffering and all, is the surest path to discovering our own center. Rohr says that we do not find our center—it finds us when we are aware of the process of living our lives in the moment and to the fullest. Rohr concludes by saying that we do not really know God except through our broken and rejoicing humanity.

PRAYER: Dear Lord, I always thought the path to enlightenment was through prayer, meditation, solitude, and the sacraments. Now I know that living life to the fullest is when we experience our deepest and most profound selves. Help me to live life that way, even during times of suffering. When I abandon myself to the mystery of Your love and grace, I come to know You the best. In Jesus' name, amen.

---

211 Richard Rohr, *Everything Belongs: The Gift of Contemplative Prayer* (New York: Crossroad, 2003), 17.

120. IS GOD ASLEEP OR ARE WE?[212]

Mark 4:38. But he was in the stern, asleep on the cushion; and they woke him up and said to him, "Teacher, do you not care that we are perishing?"

It often appears that God is absent during our difficult time. "Wake up, God," we ask. "Help us out of our difficult time! Pay attention to us! We're hurting and fearful!" We need to be reminded of a time when the disciples were yelling the same thing to Jesus in the midst of a severe storm at sea (Mark 4:37-41). Then, we must ponder if there is ever any time when God (Jesus) is not awake and attentive? His is a 24/7 job, and He is not asleep at the wheel. Rather, perhaps it is we who need awakening! "When we pray, 'Wake up, Lord', we need to be prepared for him to reply that it is we who have been asleep. Our wake-up call to God is often the moment when God's wake-up call to us is finally getting through."[213] Think about this in your difficult time. Is this a time when God can finally get through to me? Have I been so busy complaining that I have missed His call? Am I not attentive enough to the blessings that I have in the midst of my difficulties? "Part of the way the kingdom of God works is precisely by people having sudden and alarming questions raised in their minds which they will have to ponder and puzzle over."[214] God's way is not always the straightforward way or the intuitively obvious way. It must be pondered and discerned. We must constantly seek His wisdom, which is foolishness to man. See your difficult time as a wake-up call—a time to ponder and puzzle over God's plan for your life.

PRAYER: Dear Lord, I am puzzling and pondering that's for sure. But I admit that sometimes I claim that You are not being attentive, when, in fact, it is exactly the opposite: I am not paying attention. Help me to see my difficult time as an opportunity to seek Your wisdom and look for the mysterious, not necessarily the obvious. In Jesus' name, amen.

---

212   N.T. Wright, *Lent for Everyone, Mark, Year B*, 32-35; Portions paraphrased.
213   Wright, 32.
214   Wright, 32.

121. A "HIGH-LEVEL" PERSPECTIVE ON SUFFERING

2 Timothy 1:11-12a. *For this gospel I was appointed a herald and an apostle and a teacher, and for this reason I suffer as I do. But I am not ashamed, for I know the one in whom I have put my trust.*

I continue to give much thought and prayer into why we must suffer. And, today, I share a "high-level" reason: we suffer because if we didn't, we wouldn't feel the need for God nearly as much (if at all) in our lives. Just think, if everything were rosy all of the time, would you? Yes, I know, it's pleasant to think about, but wouldn't not suffering, as a constant state of being, eventually lead you to feel self-sufficient? "I don't need God; I'm in control of my life; I can handle things perfectly well on my own," you would say. Suffering brings us down a notch. Guess what? We aren't in control; there is little we can do on our own to alleviate our suffering or the human condition of suffering. We need God's help and perspective; we need something beyond ourselves to hold onto; we need hope that there is something better around the corner and that there is someone (God) who holds that hope. Maybe that doesn't give you much comfort now in your time of suffering (I told you it was a "high-level" reason), but I think it deserves consideration. Suffering is a fact of life. If there were any other way to get our attention, I think that God would have figured it out. We help our fellow suffering beings with compassion and that is pleasing to God. We pray for help to God and begin to rely on Him and that is also pleasing to God. Try to hold on to this "higher-perspective" reason (God's perspective!) during your suffering.

PRAYER: Dear Lord, I don't want to suffer. But, it is part of your plan. I'll never fully understand why people must suffer, but this "high-level" reason brings some comfort and perspective. Thank You for the compassion of other people to help me through my suffering. In Jesus' name, amen.

122. ABANDON TO JOY[215]

Matthew 25:21. *His master said to him, "Well done, good and trustworthy slave; you have been trustworthy in a few things, I will put you in charge of many things; enter into the joy of your master."*

One of the key barriers to finding and maintaining joy in our lives is the human pride that thinks we can outsmart God. Yes, it harkens back to the original sin of Adam and Eve. We can be God's equal. We can control our destiny. How misguided!! Trying to control life and manufacture happiness leads to frustration, sadness, and anger. Eventually, we come to realize that we are not in control (sometimes by going through a difficult time that we know we have no control over). Then, we can abandon ourselves into the hands of God. When we can do that without reservation, we have joy. It won't do to be guarded or half-hearted in our abandonment, holding something back "just in case." Joy won't abound in a person who holds back. It is an outpouring of the soul when it releases itself from the bondage of trying to be certain about everything, and instead recognizing that there is mystery and intrigue in this life that makes the trip worthwhile. Try to abandon the things that you are worried about into the hands of God. It is the first step to a joyful life.

PRAYER: Dear Lord, I recognize that I am still trying to be in control of my circumstances, as though I can control things on my own. Instead, help me to abandon my circumstances into Your hands, so that I might begin to know joy. In Jesus' name, amen.

---

215 John Michael Talbot, *The Lessons of St. Francis: How to Bring Simplicity and Spirituality into Your Daily Life* (New York: Dutton, 1997); Portions paraphrased.

123. AN EXCESS OF FEELING THAT IS DISPROPORTIONATE TO THE CAUSE

Luke 10:41-42. *But the Lord answered her, "Martha, Martha, you are worried and distracted by many things; there is need of only one thing. Mary has chosen the better part, which will not be taken away from her."*

We've been talking about the various ways of hearing and communicating with God, and I came across another interesting concept from James Martin, SJ[216]: God is speaking to us when the excess of feeling seems disproportionate to the cause. These can be feelings of joy or feelings of sorrow. A few examples from Martin will help to clarify this point:

You are holding an infant . . . and you are filled with a surprising sense of gratitude or awe.

You are walking along the beach, and as you cast your eyes to the horizon, you are filled with a sense of peace that is all out of proportion to what you expect.

You are out to dinner or with a friend and feel a sudden sense of contentment and you recognize how lucky you are to be blessed with her friendship.

You have finally been able to come to terms with a tragedy in your life, a sickness or death, or you find yourself consoled by a friend, and you are overcome with calm.[217]

Or, the sorrowful side:

You accompany a good friend or relative struggling with a horrible illness . . . and you feel a desperate need, an urgent longing for some comfort or connection.

---

216 James Martin, SJ, *The Jesuit Guide to (Almost) Everything: A Spirituality for Real Life* (New York: HarperCollins, 2010), 55-56; Portions paraphrased.
217 Martin, SJ, 55.

You are in the midst of a difficult time and wonder how you can ever get through the day. Then someone says something that goes straight to your heart, consoling you out of all proportion to the words, and you feel supported and loved.

You are at a funeral and wonder over the meaning of human life . . . You think, is there anyone out there aware of me, who is looking out for me?"[218]

These are examples of God communicating with you! "There is a certain expansion of the soul, a loss of inhibition, and perhaps even an increase in one's feelings of love and generosity. As well, there may even be a change in one's outlook on life, and a great sense of peace or joy."[219] It is often in the simple experiences of life that we are drawn most closely to God through the excess of feeling over what might normally be expected. Cherish those times.

PRAYER: Dear Lord, I recall times like those which have been described in this reflection, but I never attributed them to hearing/communicating with You. Help me to be more aware of Your presence when I experience this excess of feeling over what might normally be expected, and to hold onto these times reverently with a sense of calm, peace, and love. In Jesus' name, amen.

218 Martin SJ, 56.
219 Martin, SJ, 56.

124. WE CAN'T JUST 'DECIDE' TO FORGIVE[220]

Matthew 6:14. For if you forgive others their trespasses, your heavenly Father will also forgive you.

Here's an aspect of forgiveness that may surprise you: "we cannot simply 'decide' to forgive, any more than we can 'decide' to be loving."[221] We have to acknowledge God's part in the equation. Forgiveness comes from a deeper understanding of the truth of our situation. We must fully experience the depth of despair, frustration, anger, resentment, vindictiveness, hatred and desire for revenge—*without acting on these impulses.* Read that sentence again to see how it relates to you if your difficult time is one of resentment toward another person. Once we explore the background of our feelings about the person with whom we are angry and examine how these feelings are manifesting in us right now, in other words, when we are *present* to these feelings, then we begin to loosen the structures that hold our resentments in place. "Presence fills us and releases us from our bondage to the past."[222] You might then want to try the "Affirmation of Forgiveness" that proceeds like this:[223]

- I am willing to be willing to forgive those who have hurt me.*

- I am willing to forgive those who have hurt me.

- I forgive those who have hurt me.

- I see the hurt I have suffered as an opportunity to learn compassion.

- I thank God for giving me a spirit that is forgiving and compassionate.

---

220 Don Richard Riso and Russ Hudson, *The Wisdom of the Enneagram: The Complete Guide to Psychological and Spiritual Growth for the Nine Personality Types* (New York: Bantam, 1999), 350-354; Portions paraphrased.
221 Riso and Hudson, 363.
222 Riso and Hudson, 363.
223 Riso and Hudson, 362.

You may substitute a specific name of a person who has hurt you in the first three lines, and you may compose your own affirmations of other hurts, sufferings and limitations in this same style.

Forgiveness takes time, and your relationship with that person may not be restored unless the one you forgive truly repents of the way he has wronged you and also wishes to restore the relationship. Hopefully, it is of some comfort to know that forgiveness is not only a decision but is a process which is enhanced when you let "presence release you from your bondage to the past."

PRAYER: Dear Lord, I'd never thought of it that way—that forgiveness is not only a decision that I make but a process that involves You and my ability to live in the present. Help me to be willing to forgive; my first step in the "Affirmation of Forgiveness." Thank You for the forgiveness and grace You have shown me in my own circumstances. In Jesus' name, amen.

125. CREATIVITY[224]

1 Timothy 4:14-15. Do not neglect the gift that is in you, which was given to you through prophecy with the laying on of hands by the council of elders. Put these things into practice, devote yourself to them, so that all may see your progress.

Do you have a creative streak, or are you one on those persons that thinks that creativity in art, music, and literature is for the "experts"? God is the ultimate creator (just take a look at a sunset, or stare at the stars at night), and we are made in God's image. That means that we are ALL creators! Many of us have just suppressed our creativity or have become "cultural couch potatoes"—too willing to watch TV or zone out on our tablets and leave the creativity up to others. And unfortunately, much of the so-called "creativity" we watch on TV or listen to is just mass-produced garbage not worth our time to listen to—especially when we could be creating ourselves. Not musically talented? Try singing in the shower. No one will notice when you're off key, and it is a great release. Or, maybe a simple water color or a small garden, even if it hangs outside your apartment window. Once you dip your toe in the water, you may find that you enjoy creating things, and, certainly, it is a God-given talent—to everyone! "Creativity is God's gift to us. Using our creativity is our gift back to God."[225] Start by surrounding yourself with beauty: pick some flowers for your home; buy some artwork that appeals to you; listen to music that lifts your spirit. Then just create something! Your own tune or piece of poetry or literature; your own artwork; maybe learn how to throw a pot on a potter's wheel. The opportunities are endless. The benefits are untold, especially if you are going through a difficult time and are seeking a release from the rut you are in. "A Christian, above all people, should live artistically, aesthetically, and creatively. If we have been created in the image of an Artist,

---

224 John Michael Talbot, *The Lessons of St. Francis: How to Bring Simplicity and Spirituality into Your Daily Life* (New York: Dutton, 1997), 95-105; Portions paraphrased.

225 Talbot, 95; Regarding Julia Cameron in *The Artist's Way*.

then we should look for expressions of artistry and be sensitive to beauty, responsive to what has been created for our appreciation."[226]

PRAYER: Dear Lord, Maybe I have suppressed my creativity or belittled my efforts. God has placed in me an innate gift to be creative. Help me to find it and develop it. In Jesus' name, amen.

---

226 Talbot, 105; Regarding Edith Schaffer.

126. DEVELOPING A SENSE OF COMMUNITY[227]

Ephesians 6:23. *Peace be to the whole community, and love with faith, from God the Father and the Lord Jesus Christ.*

We were meant to live in community, as well as have our periods of solitude. "Community is a place of belonging, a place where people are earthed and find their identity."[228] It is hard to get a sense of yourself unless you have the comforting and objective eyes of a group of friends. As Jesus says, "For where two or three are gathered in my name, I am there among them" (Matthew 18:20). With these words, Jesus identifies a spiritual/mystical component to community that is hard to pinpoint but is uplifting. Surprisingly, it is the little things that can get in the way of community or serve as its biggest challenge. Squeezing the tube of toothpaste in the middle irritates the person who methodically squeezes from the bottom. Other little irritating habits that you notice in those you love can get in the way. I guess it's because the big things of life are tested in the little things. If we can get beyond life's little irritations, the big things have a way of taking care of themselves (thanks to God's help). Community has both an inward focus (getting along with family, being part of a small group) and an outward focus (letting others know about the importance of church and community). In your difficult time, it is especially important to develop a sense of community and be uplifted by it.

PRAYER: Dear Lord, Thank You for surrounding me with loved ones who help ground me and provide a sense of community. I realize that You are present in the midst of a gathering in some special, spiritual way that we don't fully understand. It is a source of comfort. I value my friends and loved ones and the times we share together. In Jesus' name, amen.

---

227 John Michael Talbot, *The Lessons of St. Francis: How to Bring Simplicity and Spirituality into Your Daily Life* (New York: Dutton, 1997), 130-132; Portions paraphrased.
228 Talbot, 132; Quoting Jean Vanier.

127. COMING CLEAN WITH OUR DIFFICULT TIME[229]

2 Samuel 12:7a,13a. *Nathan said to David, "You are the man!" . . . David said to Nathan, "I have sinned against the Lord."*

One of your problems with your difficult time may be "coming clean" with it. It is easier to acknowledge problems in the past, "Oh yeah, I used to be that way," than it is to confess an on-going problem. We are all sinners and have faults, but you wouldn't know it to talk to a lot of us: we put up quite a "smokescreen" of being above it all. That is why it is so important to have a few friends that you can confide in. People you can let know the real you, warts and all. As John Ortberg points out, "People are okay telling a doctor that their body has a problem or telling a mechanic that their car has a problem. Couldn't sinners be okay telling other sinners that they have a sin problem?"[230] Ortberg talks of a time when he confided all of his faults and problems to a friend, fully expecting their friendship to be damaged as a result. But, instead, it grew stronger. He concludes, "[You] can only be loved to the extent that you are known. To be fully known and fully loved is the most healing gift one human being can give another."[231] So, let down your guard, open up, and confess your sins. Jesus accepts us that way; so will our friends, and, in the process, your difficulties will have less hold over you.

PRAYER: Dear Lord, I confess that I have many sins that I attempt to hide from the world. Help me to reveal them to a trusted friend or to my pastor so that they don't keep me from being who I want to be. Certainly, You know me completely, so I am fooling no one by being secretive. I want to overcome my difficulties, and a start is to confess my sins and change my ways. In Jesus' name, amen.

---

229 John Ortberg, *The Me I Want to Be: Becoming God's Best Version of You* (Grand Rapids: Zondervan, 2009, 195-198; Portions paraphrased.
230 Ortberg, 195.
231 Ortberg, 198.

128. BEING VULNERABLE[232]

John 13:35. *By this everyone will know that you are my disciples, if you have love for one another.*

I heard a fascinating lecture today whose research concluded that there is only one variable that separates the people who have a strong sense of love and belonging and the people who really struggle for it. And that is, the people who have a strong sense of love and belonging *believe* they're *worthy* of love and belonging.[233] That's it. They believe they are worthy. Does that describe you? Or are you so mired down in your difficulties that you think that who you are, isn't enough? As Christians, we have a strong Advocate who reinforces the fact that we are worthy, that He loves us unconditionally, that we can abandon the fear and feelings of inadequacy that plague us by simply believing that we are worthy of God's love and belonging to Him. The lecturer went on to say that there is a certain amount of vulnerability required to live a healthy life: the willingness to say "I love you" first, the willingness to do something where there are no guarantees, the willingness to breathe through waiting for the doctor to call after your mammogram, the willingness to invest in a relationship that may or may not work out. Those feelings aren't pleasant, and too often, we try to numb ourselves to them. But here's a key point: you can't selectively "numb out" the bad emotions and keep just the good stuff. They go hand in hand. If we numb the bad stuff, we also numb joy, we numb gratitude, we numb happiness.[234] It takes the bad stuff to make us appreciate the good stuff. Yes, life is a roller coaster of good times and bad—recognize that you need to be fully alive to both aspects, and, during both, believe that you are worthy and enough.

PRAYER: Dear Lord, Sometimes I struggle to believe that I am worthy of Your love. And yet, in this reflection, I have learned that my sense of love and belonging depends on this belief. Help me in my struggles to be open

---

232 Brené Brown, "The Power of Vulnerability," *TED Ideas Worth Spreading,* June 12, 2010, TEDxHouston; Portions paraphrased.
233 Brown.
234 Brown.

to Your love and the love of others. And, in that openness, to be vulnerable to the good and bad that happens. Life is indeed a roller coaster of emotions, and You are the one constant I can count on in good times and bad. In Jesus' name, amen.

129. PRAYER AND ACTION[235]

2 Corinthians 8:13-14. *I do not mean that there should be relief for others and pressure on you, but it is a question of a fair balance between your present abundance and their need, so that their abundance may be for your need, in order that there may be a fair balance.*

There is a relationship between prayer and action. They complement each other; too much concentration in one area at the expense of the other leads to an imbalanced life. "Contemplation and prayer are like an oasis in a dry desert. Through prayer, we store up a huge reservoir of water. Our service is the conduit for delivering the water. But once our reservoir is depleted, we need to return to our oasis so we don't wind up stranded in the desert without water. This is a picture of the life-giving balance between prayer and service."[236] In your difficult time, you may be lacking in action; too despondent to do much. Or you may be lacking in prayer time; too depressed to pray. Try a little of both. In your prayer time, think especially of others and ways that you might be of service. Then act on what you have prayed about—perhaps serve at a local homeless shelter or volunteer to do some work on a committee at your church. There is something releasing about serving others and doing so in response to praying for them. "Any spirituality that focuses on what it does for you alone is only telling a tiny part of the whole story. Spiritual growth leads directly to service. Spirituality that doesn't is stunted and incomplete."[237]

PRAYER: Dear Lord, I am seeking balance in my spiritual life. Help me to act on my prayers. I want to model the way You lived Your life when You were on this earth with us: spending time alone in prayer, and then taking Your prayers to the people as an act of service. In Jesus' name, amen.

---

235 John Michael Talbot, *The Lessons of St. Francis: How to Bring Simplicity and Spirituality into Your Daily Life* (New York: Dutton, 1997), 189-196.
236 Talbot, 189.
237 Talbot, 196.

130. TAKE STOCK DURING ADVERSITY[238]

Romans 5:3b-4. We also boast in our sufferings, knowing that suffering produces endurance, and endurance produces character, and character produces hope.

"God isn't at work producing the circumstances you want. God is at work in bad circumstances producing the you he wants."[239] I have often heard the cliché that God will never give you more than you can handle. Some people even think that is a quote from the Bible. Not so! The Bible says that no *temptation* is given to people without a way out (1 Corinthians 10:13). But, adversity like the one you are going through in your difficult time is a different matter. The Holocaust, tornadoes, genocide, murder, poverty, and death itself are examples of adversity that are more than you can handle. We are a people who suffer, and suffering is reality—part and parcel of the human condition. What we need to do is recognize the strengthening and character building aspects of suffering. It was Ernest Hemmingway who said, "The world breaks everyone and afterward many are strong at the broken places."[240] And we all take comfort in Romans 5:3-4, "we also boast in our sufferings, knowing that suffering produces endurance, and endurance produces character, and character produces hope." You can be a "glass is half empty" person and look upon these difficult times of suffering as though they will go on forever, or you can be a "glass is half full" person and be filled with hope that our suffering builds character and is but temporary and God has good things in mind for us. Times of crisis cause us to pause and ask ourselves, "What really matters in life?" We are given the opportunity for self-reflection and analysis, and, when done properly, we become stronger, more faithful persons who cherish their relationships with other people and their God more strongly. Take stock during this time of adversity to count your blessings and grow in your faith.

PRAYER: Dear Lord, Help me to persevere in my time of difficulty and be a "glass is half full" person. There is always something that I can be thankful for in the midst of my difficulties, and I pause now to reflect on them and express my gratitude. In Jesus' name, amen.

---

238 John Ortberg, *The Me I Want to Be: Becoming God's Best Version of You* (Grand Rapids: Zondervan, 2009), 234-236; Portions paraphrased.
239 Ortberg, 237.
240 Ernest Hemmingway, *A Farewell to Arms*, 216.

131. LOVING A ROCK[241]

Job 12:7-10. *But ask the animals, and they will teach you; the birds of the air, and they will tell you; ask the plants of the earth, and they will teach you; and the fish of the sea will declare to you. Who among all these does not know that the hand of the Lord has done this? In his hand is the life of every living thing and the breath of every human being.*

Jesus spent a great deal of His time here on earth showing us how to live as humans. He realized that we had to get the humanity part of our lives right before the spiritual part would come. We must first enjoy the tangible things: love nature, marvel at the birth of a newborn, cherish our relationships with our family. The "earthy" things of life must be fully appreciated before taking on the more esoteric and harder to grasp spiritual things. "When you cannot enjoy the lilies of the field or the sparrows in the sky, don't waste time thinking you can enjoy God. Start at the bottom. Try to love a rock."[242] Is your prayer life not working for you? Having trouble relating to God? Try loving a rock. You may be feeling like you are at rock bottom anyway with your difficult time. So, get in touch with your humanity; your suffering; your tiredness over the way things are working out. By starting at the bottom and expecting nothing more than to get in touch with your humanity, you are being Christ-like.

PRAYER: Dear Lord, Help me to get in touch with my humanity. It's hard to start over at the bottom and "love a rock," but if that's what it takes to begin a spiritual journey, so be it. There is much to love about this world, and in so doing, I begin to recognize Your hand in it. In Jesus' name, amen.

---

241 Richard Rohr, *Contemplation in Action* (New York: Crossroad, 2006), 83-84; Portions paraphrased.
242 Rohr, 83-84.

132. THE WORD OF GOD IS MORE THAN JUST THE BIBLE[243]

Luke 10:17. The seventy returned with joy, saying, "Lord, in your name even the demons submit to us!"

The Word of God is more than just the Bible. True, the Bible is the written Word of God, provided to us for "teaching, for reproof, for correction and for training in righteousness, so that everyone who belongs to God may be proficient, equipped for every good work" (2 Timothy 3:15-17). But Jesus is the Living Word. When the disciples did all of the missionary work described in the book of Acts, they didn't have the guidance of the New Testament—they were *living* it, with the guidance of the Holy Spirit, given to them by Jesus. Genesis tells us that creation itself is the wondrous result of God speaking His Word and producing the earth, the cosmos, and humankind. There is incredible power in words, and we, as Christians, have the God-given ability to use words on God's behalf to enact works of grace and mercy to a hurting world. Jesus not only sent out His disciples to do His Kingdom work, but He sent out seventy people who had no special training or insight other than His authority to cast out demons and make people aware of how much God loved them and was there for them. If the seventy can do it, so can we, by God's authority in us. Your witness as a Christian can have a powerful influence on others. Your words can be Jesus' words, spoken through you. Don't underestimate the power of words; especially those words that are God-given through the power of the Holy Spirit to do good in the world. You may be going through difficulties, but you can influence others for the good by your witness and faithfulness.

PRAYER: Dear Lord, Words are powerful. Your words are precious. Help me to be Your ambassador by speaking truth to those with whom I interact. Despite my difficulties, I can be an effective witness by living out my faith and speaking the words of truth and grace that You give me. In Jesus' name, amen.

---

243 John Ortberg, *Faith and Doubt* (Grand Rapids: Zondervan, 2008), 166; Portions paraphrased.

133. NOT HEARING FROM GOD[244]

Romans 8:14. *For all who are led by the Spirit of God are children of God.*

What do we do when God is silent despite our fervent requests for an answer? Many people think that they must be doing something wrong if they do not get specific guidance from God on their requests. Instead, Dallas Willard insists that you can very well be within the perfect will of God and still not get specific answers. It just means that any of the alternatives you are trying to distinguish between are okay with God. He is allowing you to exercise your freedom of choice, while still honoring your faithfulness to Him, and His to you. After all, we are not robots, to be told exactly what to do. An amazing aspect of God's love is that He has given us free will to act and choose as we see fit. It pleases Him when we take those actions as obedient Christians seeking at all times to please God. All the proposed actions about which God is silent are perfectly in His will because none is better than the others so far as He is concerned—all are good. So, the perfect will of God may allow, for a particular person, a number of different alternatives. "People with a mature vision of God and extensive experience in his ways have no need to be obsessively anxious about doing the right thing. For the most part they will simply know what is right. But their confidence is finally not in a word from the Lord but in the Lord who is with us."[245]

PRAYER: Dear Lord, In my difficult time, I worry sometimes about Your silence when I so desperately seek answers. But, I also cherish my free will and ability to act upon alternatives in light of the awareness that any one of them will turn out for the good. Help me to remain calm and resolute in my actions, knowing that You love me and want the best for me. In Jesus' name, amen.

---

244 Dallas Willard, *Hearing God: Developing a Conversational Relationship with God* (Downers Grove: InterVarsity Press, 1984), 207-208; Portions paraphrased.
245 Willard, 208.

134. TAKING RISKS[246]

1 Kings 2:23. *Then King Solomon swore by the LORD, "So may God do to me, and more also, for Adonijah has devised this scheme at the risk of his life!"*

Are you seeking answers from God just so that you can avoid the risk of making your own decisions? God does not promise us a risk-free life. Quite the contrary: Jesus put His life on the line throughout His ministry and, ultimately, sacrificed it. The least we can do is harbor a little risk in our lives. Certainly, we don't need to seek risk on our own—it will find us. But just as certainly, we shouldn't expect that our prayers to God will cause Him to eliminate our risk. As John Boykin points out, "God does not exist to solve our problems."[247] We exist to stand up with God and count for something in His world. Risk is essential to the nature of our personal development toward maturity: only risk produces character. How boring life would be if it weren't for the element of risk and solving our problems! Don't use the lack of answers from God as your excuse not to act. God is sometimes silent to our requests because any of the alternatives we are considering are still within His perfect will. Sometimes it is uncomfortable to step out on our own when so much seems to be at risk, especially during this difficult period in your life. But in the grand scheme of things, all things work together for the good of those who believe in God (Romans 8:28), so go ahead—take the plunge!

PRAYER: Dear Lord, Life can be a risky proposition, and sometimes it feels like I am "hanging out" on my own without the necessary guidance. But, I have to have faith that what I am facing works out ultimately for Your good and to proceed with the best course of action that I think is consistent with what I have learned about You. In Jesus' name, amen.

---

246 Dallas Willard, *Hearing God: Developing a Conversational Relationship with God* (Downers Grove: InterVarsity Press, 1984), 210-211; Portions paraphrased.
247 Willard, 211; As quoted by the author.

135. THE BEATITUDES[248]

Matthew 5:3. Blessed are the poor in spirit, for theirs is the kingdom of heaven.

We are all familiar with the Beatitudes, Jesus' treatise on the Good News of life in the kingdom (Matthew 5:1-12). But too many of us think of the Beatitudes as Jesus' pronouncement on how we should live our lives—kind of a manual on what we should do to inherit the Kingdom: "try hard to live like this." Instead, N.T. Wright asserts that the Beatitudes are for the downtrodden and disadvantaged people of Jesus' day (and today!) who aren't living in the mainstream of society, where power and prestige and position in the "pecking order" are what's important. So, it's not, "Blessed are the poor in spirit"—"Oh, that means that I need to be poor in spirit to receive God's blessings." Or, "Blessed are the mourners"—"Oh, that means I have to mourn in order to receive God's blessing." No, the Beatitudes are not a set of rules to emulate; they are an announcement to those who are already like that (poor in spirit or mourning) that they are okay, that the Kingdom of Heaven is for them. It is Good News, not Good Advice. So, don't beat yourself up for not being able to live up to the Beatitudes, nevertheless understand them. They are an indicator to those who are already in difficult circumstances (like you) that the Good News is for them in particular.

PRAYER: Dear Lord, I've been having trouble trying to live up to the message of the Beatitudes. Thank You for this interpretation, which helps me to understand that Jesus' message of love and blessing is for me and others in our present condition. We have nothing to "live up to" other than basking in Your love and reflecting Your love to others. In Jesus' name, amen.

---

248 N.T. Wright, *Lent for Everyone: Luke, Year C* (Louisville: Westminster John Knox Press, 2012), 21-22; Portions paraphrased.

136. GETTING COMFORTABLE WITH SOLITUDE

Revelation 8:1. *When the Lamb opened the seventh seal, there was silence in heaven for about half an hour.*

How are you doing in spending time alone with God? "By practicing the discipline of solitude, we are creating a space in our lives where God can be with us. And over time, as that space grows, so can our relationship with the living God."[249] We are so caught up in the "busyness" of life that we are uncomfortable with solitude. "We seem so frightened today of being alone that we never let it happen . . . We choke the space with continuous music, chatter, and companionship to which we do not even listen. It is simply there to fill the vacuum. When the noise stops there is no inner music to take its place."[250] Silence is beautiful. It is a primary way that God communicates with us. Learn to carve out times of solitude and get comfortable with the silence. "For [St. Francis of Assisi] and other saints, monastics, and mystics down through the ages, the desire for solitude isn't an effort to flee from the world; it's an attempt to run toward God, to know God better, and to hear God's voice amid the din."[251] I like the thought that in silence and solitude, we are "running toward God." God pervades the silence with His presence, and we must be deliberate in our attempt to create times of silence to commune with Him.

PRAYER: Dear Lord, Help me to get comfortable with solitude and silence. I too often get caught up in being so busy that I don't take time out to commune with You. Let me spend a little time after reading this reflection to be quiet and meditate and find You. In Jesus' name, amen.

---

249 John Michael Talbot, *The Lessons of St. Francis: How to Bring Simplicity and Spirituality into Your Daily Life* (New York: Dutton, 1997), 66.
250 Talbot, 56; Quoting Anne Morrow Lindberg.
251 Talbot, 58.

137. GOD IN THE SIMPLE THINGS[252]

2 Kings 5:11. But Naaman became angry and went away, saying, "I thought that for me he would surely come out, and stand and call on the name of the LORD his God, and would wave his hand over the spot, and cure the leprosy!"

In Reflection 123, we talked about how having an excess of feeling which is disproportionate to the cause is a form of communicating with God. "Much in Western culture tries to tamp down or even deny these naturally spiritual experiences and explain them away in purely rational terms. It's chalked up to something other than God."[253] The story of Naaman in 2 Kings 5:1-19 is like that. Naaman, a famous army commander, was told by Elisha that to be healed of his leprosy, he needed to wash himself in the Jordan River seven times to be cured. Naaman is incensed. Shouldn't an important person like him be bathed in a more important river? He eventually complies and is healed. God often works via simple means rather than the spectacular. That is why you should not discount a "simple" experience during your difficult time as being not from God. You may even be fearful to admit that God is speaking to you. "Religious experiences are often dismissed not out of doubt that they aren't real, but out of fear that they are real after all."[254] Don't miss out on this opportunity to recognize the work of God in your life. Embrace the emotion that fills a void in your life beyond over what might be normally expected, as coming from God.

PRAYER: Dear Lord, Please help me to be more attuned to the times when You might be speaking to me, and to not rationalize them as "just emotion." Help me to discern the times when You are communicating with me and to act upon what I hear. In Jesus' name, amen.

---

252 James Martin, SJ, *The Jesuit Guide to (Almost) Everything: A Spirituality for Real Life* (New York: HarperCollins, 2010), 68-70; Portions paraphrased.
253 Martin, SJ, 66-67.
254 Martin, SJ, 69.

138. THE THREE DOMES OF MEANING

Colossians 3:4. *When Christ who is your life is revealed, then you also will be revealed with him in glory.*

Richard Rohr likes to talk about three "domes of meaning": each successive dome encompasses the previous one. The first dome is "My story," where we think about our particular circumstances and try to understand ourselves as individuals like the talk-show hosts do. This is the dome that we most often reside in during our difficult time. The second is "Our story," where we regard ourselves as part of a group: our gender, our ethnicity, our religion, our occupation, etc. It is historically the way that most people have seen themselves and tend to defend their group so vigorously, even to the point of conflict and war. The third dome is "The Story," which is God's revelation to us: the patterns that are always true, for example, that forgiveness heals, or love is love regardless of your faith background and tradition. "The genius of the biblical revelation is that [we have] permission and even direction to take conscious ownership of our own story at every level, every part of our life and experience. God will use all of this material, even the negative parts of our difficult time, to bring us to life and love."[255] We can see ourselves as people of the Big Picture, while still relishing all of the mystery and intricacy of our individual and group stories and know that God has a way of integrating it all to bring out the fullness of life. Jesus taught us to call that the Kingdom of God.

PRAYER: Dear Lord, Help me to see my life in the context of the Big Picture, where I can rest with the assurance that You are making sense out of the various pieces of my life—even the negative parts. I tend to live in the dome of "my story" and place too great an emphasis on how I should be the center of attention, when, in fact, there is a grander aspect to life that is under Your loving control, where everything comes together and makes sense. I humbly seek that perspective. In Jesus' name, amen.

---

255 Richard Rohr, *Things Hidden: Scripture as Spirituality* (Cincinnati: St. Anthony Messenger Press), 432.

139. THE MYSTERY OF THE TRINITY

Luke 1:41-42. *When Elizabeth heard Mary's greeting, the child leaped in her womb. And Elizabeth was filled with the Holy Spirit and exclaimed with a loud cry, "Blessed are you among women, and blessed is the fruit of your womb."*

We tend to focus on the three persons of the Trinity (Father, Son, and Holy Spirit) separately, and then marvel at the mystery that they can be three-in-one. Richard Rohr points out that it is the *relationship* between the three that is important. He quotes Richard of Saint Victor, who says, "For God to be good, God can be one. For God to be loving, God has to be two because love is always a relationship. For God to be supreme joy and happiness, God has to be three. Lovers do not know full happiness until they both delight in the same thing, like new parents with the ecstasy of their first child."[256] We experience joy when someone not only likes us but loves the same things that we do. It gives us a basis upon which to build a solid relationship. So it is with the Trinity. Imagine the Father and the Son sharing the mutual love of the Holy Spirit and being excited and filled with joy about the creation. Richard Rohr says that the Holy Spirit is whatever the Father and the Son are excited about—about everything in creation! Relationships are so important in helping us through our journey of life. In your difficult time, be sure to surround yourself with a good network of friends and family—you are modeling the Trinity!

PRAYER: Dear Lord, I do tend to view the Father, the Son, and the Holy Spirit separately. It is hard to fathom them as one. But I like the thought that they are in relationship to one another and that they are experiencing mutual joy and excitement over their creation, of which we are a cherished part. So much so that they are one. I'm excited to model that relationship in my own life. In Jesus' name, amen.

---

256 Richard Rohr, "The Shape of God: Deepening the Mystery of the Trinity." CD. Albuquerque: Center for Contemplation and Action, 2004.

140. A CALL TO HOLINESS[257]

Philippians 2:22. *But Timothy's worth you know, how like a son with a father he has served with me in the work of the gospel.*

One of the ways God calls us to holiness is through the example of other Christians, past and present. From the saints and mystics of old, we are inspired by stories that make us want to be like them. Stories that sometimes seem so beyond our experience base that we wonder if they really occurred, but, in faith, we try to put ourselves in their shoes and marvel at the way God worked in their lives and wonder if God can work in our lives the same way. Did Peter really walk on water? Did Jesus really turn water into wine? Did Julian of Norwich really have an encounter with Jesus when she was sick onto death that sustained and uplifted her and changed her life?[258] So many wondrous stories that give us hope for God to perform similar works of grace in our lives. But, we need look no further than today's "saints" if we want to be inspired. They are the objects of our affection that draw us closer to God or, maybe it is better to say, that open us up so that God can more fully enter our lives. Do you love your wife and children dearly? You can experience the love of God through them. Do you cherish a relationship with a best friend? Find God there. Do you love to take walks in the woods and admire God's creation? It is an opportunity to commune with God. Are you enamored with art or music? God is there, too. It is through the ordinary interaction with other people, and, in particular, a real desire to emulate the lives of the people who you admire and consider to be "holy" that God calls you to holiness. Avail yourselves to these opportunities for holiness through interaction with humanity to aid you through your difficult time. As James Martin, SJ, says, "Holiness always makes its home in humanity."[259] So seek out the counsel of others whom you admire, and, through them, find God calling you to holiness.

---

257 James Martin, SJ, *The Jesuit Guide to (Almost) Everything: A Spirituality for Real Life* (New York: HarperCollins, 2010), 76-77; Portions paraphrased.
258 Julian of Norwich, *Revelations of Divine Love* (New York: Penguin Books, 1999), 6-12.
259 Martin,SJ, 77.

PRAYER: Dear Lord, There are several people whom I admire and want to emulate. Not that they are perfect—no human is—but because they exhibit traits that remind me of how Jesus lived and would have responded to things. Help me to learn from the saints of old and from present day "saints," so that I can open myself to Your call of holiness. In Jesus' name, amen.

141. NOTHING CAN SEPARATE US FROM GOD'S LOVE[260]

2 Thessalonians 3:3. *But the Lord is faithful; he will strengthen and guard you from the evil one.*

"When the going gets tough, the tough get going." There is perhaps some wisdom in this adage, if the "getting going" includes God in the picture. We know very well that Christians aren't exempt from difficulties in this world. You are reading these reflections because you are going through a difficult time and need some relief and guidance. The relief and guidance in a nutshell is this: "None of the things that happen to you, none of the troubles you encounter have any power to get between you and God, dilute his grace in you, or dilute his will from you."[261] Eugene Peterson asserts, yes, you will have troubles, but they will not separate you from the love of God, and they will not allow evil purposes to come between you and God. How is this possible? Because of God's providence, His very nature is love. No, He can't come and rescue you from every problem that besets you. On this earth, He has given us freedom to pursue our dreams, and, in that freedom, comes the possibility that we will proverbially stub our toe. Expecting God to come to our rescue for every little thing would be like asking a famous surgeon to drop everything he is doing in the operating room to put iodine on a scratch.[262] Nevertheless, the same faith that works in big things works in little things—the "things" of life happen, but God protects us from them turning into evil. Instead, we turn to Scripture and learn about God. Our help comes from God, not from the "things." Praise God for His creation and the freedom He gives us to enjoy it in our own unique way. He made everything, and we don't need to turn to the "things" of life for help; we need to turn to Him. "[God's promise] is not that we shall never stub our toes, but that no injury, no illness no accident, no distress will have evil power over us, that is, will be able to

---

260 Eugene H. Peterson, *A Long Obedience in the Same Direction: Discipleship in an Instant Society* (Downers Grove: InterVarsity Press, 1980), 38-41; Portions paraphrased.
261 Peterson, 39.
262 Peterson, 40.

separate us from God's purposes in us."[263] Having trouble? Yes, indeed get going, but with God at the helm.

PRAYER: Dear Lord, Help me to trust in Your providence. I am fully aware that Christians aren't exempt from troubles. I am in the midst of trouble right now. But, it is comforting to know that my troubles can't separate me from You or Your ultimate plan for good in my life. In Jesus' name, amen.

---

263 Eugene H. Peterson, *A Long Obedience in the Same Direction: Discipleship in an Instant Society* (Downers Grove: InterVarsity Press, 1980), 38.

142. ABOUT NATURAL DISASTERS

Acts 16:26. Suddenly there was an earthquake, so violent that the foundations of the prison were shaken; and immediately all the doors [to the prison] were opened and everyone's chains were unfastened.

Is it the will of God that we suffer as a result of natural disasters and sicknesses? According to Shirley Guthrie "Yes and no."[264] Yes, in that God has set in motion natural laws that play out according to barometric highs and lows and viruses and germs, but, no, in the sense that it is not His specific will to produce a hurricane or sickness at a given place or point in time for a specific reason. Shirley Guthrie puts it into marvelous perspective this way: "The God of scripture is a living personal God who is present and at work in our lives to lead the way, set free, forgive, help and save—not just cause, program and determine everything that happens from above. Christians guided by scripture, then, seek to understand what God wills for their lives and is doing in their lives by listening to what the Bible tells us about who God is and what God does, not by trying to figure it out for ourselves by assuming that God is the hidden cause behind everything that happens."[265] So don't blame God for your difficult time; blame the evil circumstances that still surround us, which God is in the process of overcoming through Christ. God cares deeply about what you are going through—He loves us unconditionally with a love that is evident when you read the Bible and interact with other Christians.

PRAYER: Dear Lord, What a marvelous world You have created! And yet, in the grand scheme of things, natural disasters and sicknesses are real and with us. You don't specifically will them upon us; in fact, quite the contrary—You love us and want what is best for us. Let that be a source of comfort to us in our difficult time. In Jesus' name, amen.

---

264 Shirley C. Guthrie, *Christian Doctrine* (Louisville: Westminster John Knox, 1994, 170.
265 Guthrie, 171.

143. CLOSENESS TO GOD

Mark 12:42-44. *A poor widow came and put in two small copper coins, which are worth a penny. Then he [Jesus] called his disciples and said to them, "Truly I tell you, this poor widow has put in more than all those who are contributing to the treasury. For all of them have contributed out of their abundance; but she out of her poverty has put in everything she had, all she had to live on."*

The Bible shows that Jesus spent a lot of time with the poor. Certainly, they are the downtrodden of life and deserve attention, but sometimes it puzzled me, in light of God's unconditional love for everyone, why He would single out the poor for preferential treatment. Shouldn't God hear the cry of everyone? And then came this insight from James Martin, SJ, "Less stands between the [poor] and God. Overall, they are more aware of their dependence on God. So . . . they are able to place themselves close to God: the poor have less between them and God, the poor rely on God, the poor make God their friend, and the poor are often more grateful to God. And so, God is close to them."[266] Likewise, you may be drawn closer to God because you are impoverished in some way by your difficult time. Relish this opportunity to be close to God, employing some of the prayer methods that we have been learning.

PRAYER: Dear Lord, I can see why there is less "baggage" between You and the poor, and how they (and me in my difficult time) might be closer to You. Help me to simplify my life so that I have less between me and You and can draw closer to You. In Jesus' name, amen.

---

266 James Martin, SJ, *The Jesuit Guide to (Almost) Everything: A Spirituality for Real Life* (New York: HarperCollins, 2010), 201.

144. GOD IS OUR HELP

Psalm 124:8. Our help is in the name of the Lord, who made heaven and earth.

"Faith develops out of the most difficult aspects of our existence, not the easiest."[267] If you can embrace that statement by Eugene Peterson, then you can get through your difficult time. In fact, if you have the apostle Paul's perspective, you will be able to rejoice in your difficult time: "we also boast in our sufferings, knowing that suffering produces endurance, and endurance produces character, and character produces hope" (Romans 5:3-4). OK, so maybe we're not as strong (or optimistic) as Paul was, but it is important to see that God is our source of strength in difficult times, and we can witness to that fact rather than feel sorry for ourselves. Look to the example of other Christians. The exemplary ones are giving witness to their faith by telling stories—either their own story of how God has helped them through a difficult time or a story from the Bible about how God came to the rescue of His people. Still having trouble? Read the Psalms. They are the best representations of how the writer (principally David) was in dire straits but acknowledged his Lord as his Deliverer. When I went through my frightening experience of cancer and chemotherapy, I read a Psalm each night before going to bed. It was a tremendous source of inspiration and faith. If the Psalmist could go through "the valley of the shadow of death," then so could I! Take Psalm 124 for example:

It does not argue God's help; it does not explain God's help; it is a testimony of God's help in the form of a song. The song is so vigorous, so confident, so bursting with what can only be called reality, that it fundamentally changes our approach and our questions. No longer does it seem the highest priority to ask, "Why did this happen to me? Why do I feel left in the lurch?" Instead we ask, "How does it happen that there are people who sing with such confidence, 'God is our help'?"[268]

---

267 Eugene H. Peterson, *A Long Obedience in the Same Direction: Discipleship in an Instant Society* (Downers Grove: InterVarsity Press, 1980), 74.
268 Peterson, 68.

It is the witness of others who praise God despite the difficulties of life that buoys us up. Be one of those people! Better yet, be one of a group of those people—your fellow churchgoers, who, with you in worship and in prayer, can lift your spirits.

PRAYER: Dear Lord, Help me to be a witness to Your good works rather than feel sorry for myself. You never promised that my life as a Christian would be easy—only that You and my fellow Christians would be with me through my difficulties. When I falter, I have the Psalms and the redemptive stories in the Bible and of other Christians to count on. Thank You for their witness. Help me also to praise You and be Your witness despite my difficult time. In Jesus' name, amen.

145. BARRIERS TO FRIENDSHIP

1 Chronicles 12:17b. *But if you have come to betray me to my adversaries, though my hands have done no wrong, then may the God of our ancestors see and give judgment.*

Let us discuss some barriers to friendship based on the advice of James Martin, SJ.[269] First, possessiveness—no one wants a "clingy" friend who doesn't leave you alone to be your own person. You need to give your friend the freedom to grow and change. Second, overactivity—you let yourself become too busy to pay attention to your friend. Third, excessive emotional involvement—you focus too much on your feelings and analyze every slight and comment. You are too "clingy" and don't give the relationship room to breathe. Fourth, competition—is your friend's success a threat to your own self-worth? Fifth, envy—coveting what your friend has masks your own blessings that you should be thankful for. Finally, harboring a complaint-driven relationship where getting together is just an excuse for carping and complaining about life. If the complaints and disagreements of this last barrier involve drugs or alcohol abuse, you must put an end to these relationships and help the person seek professional help or group therapy. Perhaps these barriers have struck a chord with you in some of the friendships you have. Perhaps they remind you of things to avoid during your difficult time. By overcoming these barriers, you can develop successful, healthy friendships.

PRAYER: Dear Lord, I am striving to maintain healthy friendships in my life, and I will keep these barriers in mind so that I can avoid them. Help me to value my friendships and not get caught up in possessiveness, being "too busy," getting too emotionally involved, being overly competitive or jealous, or condoning substance abuse. Thank You for the friends that I have. In Jesus' name, amen.

---

269 James Martin, SJ, *The Jesuit Guide to (Almost) Everything: A Spirituality for Real Life* (New York: HarperCollins, 2010), 246-248.

146. DOWNWARD MOBILITY[270]

2 Kings 19:30. *The surviving remnant of the house of Judah shall again take root downward, and bear fruit upward.*

We are so focused on the success path that we miss Christ's call of downward mobility. This is a phrase used by Henri Nouwen to capture the thought that the way of God's progression in our lives is not upward, but downward, as hard as that is to swallow. God became incarnate in Jesus, a downward move to live and breathe among us; Jesus went into the wilderness, a downward move to be tempted by Satan; Jesus lived a life of simplicity among the poor and the lepers, a downward move of humility; and Jesus suffered and died on the cross, the ultimate downward move on our behalf. Where does God ever talk positively about striving for success, "climbing the ladder," "doing better than the Joneses," or seeking power and prestige? Those are the ways of the world. Not that it is wrong to seek progress in our lives and try to improve ourselves, as long as they are not our main objective in life.

Deep in our hearts we already know success, fame, influence, power and money do not give us the inner joy and peace we crave. Somewhere we can sense a certain envy of those who have shed all false ambitions and found a deeper fulfillment in their relationship with God. Somewhere we can get a taste of that mysterious joy in the smile of those who have nothing to lose. Then we begin to perceive the downward road is not the road to hell, but the road to heaven.[271]

Perhaps your difficult time is just a manifestation of the downward path that is so necessary to live to find Christ. Embrace your feelings of despair and grief and suffering and, through them, find faith and the strength to press on.

PRAYER: Dear Lord, I am somewhat disheartened to come to grips with this path of downward mobility. On the surface, how much better things appear if we could just let our upwardly mobile society dictate our path. But, true peace and joy comes from embracing your path of simplicity and suffering. Help me to embrace it. In Jesus' name, amen.

---

270 Henri Nouwen, *The Selfless Way of Christ: Downward Mobility and the Spiritual Life* (London: Darton, Longman and Todd, 2007), 33-35; Portions paraphrased.
271 Nouwen, 34.

147. MORE ON THE DOWNWARD WAY

Psalm 34:18. *The LORD is near to the brokenhearted, and saves the crushed in spirit.*

To continue yesterday's discussion of the downward way, Henri Nouwen emphasizes, "The Holy Spirit leads us on the downward way, not to cause us to suffer or to subject us to pain and humiliation, but rather to help us to see God present in the midst of our struggles."[272] He says that there are three temptations which follow the way of upward mobility and cause us to return to the ways of the world: the temptation to be relevant, the temptation to be spectacular, and the temptation to be powerful. The temptation to be relevant means that we believe that we are what we produce. It may even feel like it is our "call," but it isn't when it becomes the all-consuming passion of our life. The temptation to be spectacular means that we want to force God to pay attention to the unusual, the sensational, the extraordinary, the unheard of; and then to force people to believe. We pay attention to the statistics of growth and visibility and notoriety and pretend that they are the main criteria of the value we are producing. The temptation to be powerful is perhaps the most seductive and may involve the quest for money, connections, fame, intellectual ability, and skills. It is seductive because you can never get enough of it: it escalates into more and more craving for more and more power. Nouwen says the true path is one of powerlessness: "We are called to speak to people not where they have it together, but where they are aware of their pain, not where they are in control but where they are trembling and insecure, not where they are self-assured and assertive, but where they dare to doubt and raise hard questions; in short, not where they live in the illusion of immortality, but where they are ready to face their broken, mortal and fragile humanity."[273] Are you beginning to understand downward mobility? Is it a comfort to you in your difficult time? Downward mobility requires an undivided attention to God.

PRAYER: Dear Lord, I admit that I sometimes succumb to the temptations of being relevant, spectacular, and powerful. And, why not? They are the

---

272 Henri Nouwen, *The Selfless Way of Christ: Downward Mobility and the Spiritual Life* (London: Darton, Longman and Todd, 2007), 47.
273 Nouwen, 63.

success criteria of the world. But, Christians are held to a different standard of humility, love, and service and may very well suffer in the course of it. In fact, I'm suffering through trying to realize how the standard of downward mobility relates to me in my difficult time. Help me to get comfortable with downward mobility. In Jesus' name, amen.

148. THINKING GREAT THOUGHTS[274]

Philippians 1:7. *It is right for me to think this way about all of you, because you hold me in your heart, for all of you share in God's grace with me, both in my imprisonment and in the defense and confirmation of the gospel.*

"People who live great lives are people who habitually think great thoughts."[275] Keep this in mind when you get down on yourself, like you're probably doing during your difficult time. You can *think* your way out of your difficulties! Nobody can control what you think except you. John Milton, in his epic poem, *Paradise Lost,* said, "The mind is its own place, and in it self/ Can make a Heav'n of Hell, a Hell of Heav'n."[276] We need to be in the business of thinking heavenly thoughts. God enables them through the Holy Spirit. When you find yourself thinking negatively, say, "Holy Spirit, would You help me? Would You give me the right thoughts?" Memorizing key verses of Scripture also helps. You can bring them to mind when you start feeling down. According to John Ortberg, you can't tell yourself to stop thinking negative thoughts—it immediately brings to mind the very thoughts you are trying to stop. Instead, listen for another voice—God's voice, which is spoken through "silent nudging," through the helpful insights of other Christians, and through what we read—especially Scripture. It takes practice not to get down on yourself, especially when you are going through a difficult time. But, think great thoughts, and rise above your problems and negativity.

PRAYER: Dear Lord, I often catch myself thinking negative thoughts, and, when I tell myself not to, it takes me deeper into them. Help me to seek another voice—Your voice—and to put myself in the presence of other Christians who can lift my spirits and help me to begin thinking great thoughts. In Jesus' name, amen.

---

274 John Ortberg, *The Me I Want to Be: Becoming God's Best Version of You* (Grand Rapids: Zondervan, 2009), 89-90; Paraphrased.
275 Ortberg, 90.
276 John Milton, *Paradise Lost,* Lines 233-234.

149. THE PASCHAL MYSTERY[277]

Luke 23:46. Then Jesus, crying with a loud voice, "Father, into your hands I commend my spirit." Having said this, he breathed his last.

So, at this point in our journey, have you begun to realize that your suffering, your difficult time, is part of what is called the "paschal mystery"? It is somehow a vital part of life—a condition of life without which there would be little meaning and purpose? Christ Himself exhibited the ultimate form of this suffering, and His death on the cross is His way of saying, "love and pay the price for it." "The cross is not the price that Jesus *had* to pay to talk God into loving us. It is simply where love will lead us. Jesus names the agenda. If we love, if we give ourselves to feel the pain of the world, it will crucify us."[278] It is very humbling to realize this. It is also very releasing. Pain, suffering, poverty, and, yes, abandonment are vital to life. If we can hold the tension and the essentially tragic nature of human existence within us, we will know Christ and Him crucified. We will know what it is to live life to the fullest extent that God has in mind. We will see the crucifixion as the worst thing in human history and the best thing in human history—the price we pay for holding together the paradoxes of life; the tension between good and bad, of death and rebirth, of Christ's crucifixion and resurrection. And, it is the ultimate triumph of goodness and resurrection that gives us hope, that enables us to "bear the cross" in this life. Hold on to your difficult time. Learn from it. Embrace it as an integral part of life.

PRAYER: Dear Lord, I never thought of my difficult time as part of Jesus' agenda, as part of the price we pay to love and love fully. It's still hard to go through, and I wish it would "go away," but now I have the perspective that it is a basic part of life which ultimately leads to growth and hope as we see Your ultimate triumph. In Jesus' name, amen.

---

277 Richard Rohr, *Everything Belongs: The Gift of Contemplative Prayer* (New York: Crossroad, 2003), 170-173; Portions paraphrased.
278 Rohr, 169.

150. OBEDIENCE

Romans 1:4-5. Jesus Christ our Lord, through whom we have received grace and apostleship to bring about the obedience of faith among all the Gentiles for the sake of his name.

I've always thought of obedience in a slightly negative way: doing what we might not otherwise do on our own to satisfy someone else's demands or wishes. But, James Martin, SJ, gave me another angle: obedience is about freedom. "It frees you from excessive self-interest, careerism, and pride and allows you to respond more readily to the larger needs of the community."[279] I would add that it frees people going through a difficult time from excessive focus on their hardship. "Rather than wondering, 'What's the best way for me to get ahead?', obedience asks you to trust that your superiors, who presumably have a better idea of larger needs, will be able to answer another question: 'What's the best use of this man's talents, given the needs of the community?'"[280] What an interesting "spin" on obedience! In your difficult time, you may not consider anything very freeing, least of all obedience. But, maybe rather than obsessing about your own negative situation, you need to think instead about freeing yourself up to be obedient. There are undoubtedly service needs within your church or prayer requests that you have heard that someone asks you to pray for—anything that will take you out of your preoccupation with your own predicament and let you consider the needs of others—the freedom of obedience.

PRAYER: Dear Lord, I never thought of obedience as freeing, but this reflection has given me a new perspective. Help me to be obedient to Your call to serve and, in so doing, to reap the personal benefit of forgetting about my own predicament. In Jesus' name, amen.

---

279 James Martin, SJ, *The Jesuit Guide to (Almost) Everything: A Spirituality for Real Life* (New York: HarperCollins, 2010), 270.
280 Martin, SJ, 270.

151. WHAT WILL OUR RESURRECTED BODIES BE LIKE?[281]

John 20:26. *A week later his disciples were in the house, and Thomas was with them. Although the doors were shut, Jesus came and stood among them and said, "Peace be with you!"*

We Christians believe in *bodily* resurrection. That means, at the second coming of Christ, we will have bodies—we will not exist in some spiritual, ephemeral state, floating in the clouds. We don't have a very good clue as to what these resurrected bodies will look like—the disciples were trying to describe something for which they didn't have very good language. What clues we have comes from the New Testament observations of what Jesus looked like in His resurrected body. It was physical in that it could be touched; His wounds recognized, and He ate. But it also had the mysterious properties of being able to walk through locked doors and appear suddenly. The men on the road to Emmaus didn't readily recognize Him, so your physical appearance may be different (improved). Revelation tells us that there will be no more pain, no more suffering, no more decay, and no more death. We clearly have a new, magnificent body to look forward to. We can reflect on what it will be like then and, perhaps, diminish some of our worries about our difficult times or the state of our bodies now.

PRAYER: Dear Lord, It is good to imagine what my resurrected body will be like. I am going through a difficult time right now, and I need all the help I can get. The promise of a future life here on earth where there is no more pain, suffering, decay, or death is comforting and a source of hope. May it sustain me now. In Jesus' name, amen.

---

281 N.T. Wright, *Surprised by Hope: Rethinking Heaven, the Resurrection, and the Mission of the Church* (New York: HarperOne, 2008), 158-160; Portions paraphrased.

152. GOD IS DEVASTATED BY OUR SUFFERING[282]

1 Samuel 9:16b. For I have seen the suffering of my people, because their outcry has come to me.

We've talked at some length about suffering and have concluded that we will never fully understand why we suffer any more than we will fully understand the mystery of God. Suffering is part of life; it was part of Christ's life, and we must enter into it obediently while trying to see God's purposes in the midst of it. James Martin, SJ, describes a painful wrist problem that limited his ability to write and type. His superior asked him to identify where God was in all of this, and he had great difficulty. But, he finally realized that since he could type for only short periods of time each day, he was more grateful for what he was able to write and more intentional about what he wrote. He was more patient and less likely to be prideful. And, he was more aware of others with limitations and far graver illnesses. That is not to say that we can always find God in our suffering. Senseless killings, babies dying, the suffering of the innocent, defy our logic. But, in our suffering, we are often able to meet God in new ways—perhaps because our guard is down, and we are more open to God's presence. Ultimately, suffering is something that each of us must come to grips with personally. Hopefully, we will recognize that God is devastated by our suffering and wants desperately to console us. We can look to Jesus as the ultimate example of suffering and be consoled in His ultimate triumph.

PRAYER: Dear Lord, I don't want to suffer, but it is an inevitable part of life. Help me to learn from my suffering and to attempt to see Your purposes in it. I know that You are devastated by my suffering and are a consoling presence when I come to You in my pain and discomfort. In Jesus' name, amen.

---

282 James Martin, SJ, *The Jesuit Guide to (Almost) Everything: A Spirituality for Real Life* (New York: HarperCollins, 2010); Portions paraphrased.

153. COMPASSION FOR A DIFFICULT PERSON[283]

Genesis 45:4-5. Then Joseph said to his brothers, "Come closer to me." And they came closer. He said, "I am your brother, Joseph, whom you sold into Egypt. And now do not be distressed, or angry with yourselves, because you sold me here; for God sent me before you to preserve life."

Sometimes God puts difficult people in our path. It may not seem like it at the time, but it is a method of helping us to grow. The difficult person can "draw out" of you characteristics that you didn't know you had, like compassion, patience, longsuffering. The usual tendency is quite the opposite: we may get angry with the person, impatient, try to "brush him off." But, when we see that God has a purpose in putting difficult people in our lives, it can change us for the better. Recall the story of Joseph, whose brothers were so jealous of him that they sold him into slavery (Genesis 37, 42-43). Later, Joseph became the Prime Minister of Egypt, to whom his brothers must come to seek food during a famine. They do not recognize Joseph, so he puts them to the test, falsely accusing the youngest son Benjamin of stealing Joseph's prized silver cup, for which the penalty is death. One of the other brothers offers to take Benjamin's place, so concerned is he for his brother's safety and knowing that he is a favorite son of their father. Once Joseph realizes that his brothers have had a change of heart, he is filled with compassion towards them and reconciles with them. If Joseph can have compassion on those who tried to destroy him, you can have compassion on someone you are going through difficulties with. Maybe it's the "root cause" of your difficult time. It takes patience; it takes some help of prayer and intervention of the Holy Spirit, but it can be done.

PRAYER: Dear Lord, Fill me with compassion for those with whom I am having a difficult time. Help me to see that they have been placed in my path to help me grow. It is difficult to be kind to someone that I don't like, and I can't do it on my own. I will pray about it and let Your love and compassion flow over into my circumstances. In Jesus' name, amen.

---

283 John Ortberg, *The Me I Want to Be: Becoming God's Best Version of You* (Grand Rapids: Zondervan, 2009), 210-218; Portions paraphrased.

154. SILENCE IS THE LANGUAGE OF GOD

Deuteronomy 27:9a. *Then Moses and the levitical priests spoke to all Israel, saying: Keep silence and hear, O Israel!*

"Silence is the language of God, and the only language deep enough to absorb all the contradictions and failures that we are holding against ourselves. God loves us silently, because God has no case to make against us. Silent communion absorbs our self-hatred, as every lover knows."[284] I hope that you are carving out silent time with God. It is His favorite form of communication. There is something about silently communing with God that is very calming and reassuring. As you know, I meditate silently twice a day using the method of Centering Prayer (see Reflection 20). "Silence is the ability to trust that God is acting, teaching, and using me—even before I perform, or after my seeming failures. Silence is the necessary space around things that allows them to develop and flourish without my pushing."[285] So much of life seems to involve "pushing" and trying to force things to happen our way according to our timing. How much better to put some space around things by being silent before God. It takes the "rush" out of life and cushions it with a higher regard for the things of God, who is never in a rush. The next time you are feeling panicky or rushed or overwhelmed by your difficult time, stop for a few minutes and be silent. You will benefit from it.

PRAYER: Dear Lord, I seem to always be in a rush and pushing to get things done. Help me to carve out times of silence before You to get things back in balance in my life and to regard things from Your perspective. In Jesus' name, amen.

---

284 Richard Rohr, *Simplicity: The Art of Letting Go* (New York: Crossroads, 2004), 97.
285 Richard Rohr, *Contemplation in Action* (New York: Crossroad, 2006), 134.

155. THE JESUS PRAYER

The Jesus Prayer. *Lord, Jesus Christ, Son of God, have mercy on me, a sinner.*[286]

Many people find that repeating a meditational phrase over and over is calming and helpful. One that is often selected is "The Jesus Prayer" that repeats the phrase, "Lord, Jesus Christ, Son of God, have mercy on me, a sinner." One of the desert fathers (a group of Christians who fled to the desert to worship as they wanted around 300 AD) went to his mentor and said, "I have repeated the phrase many times, but do not see any benefit." His mentor said, "Repeat it 1000 more times and see if that helps." I have used this phrase myself and been comforted by it, although I am a bigger fan of the Centering Prayer method described in Reflection 20. When you pick a phrase, stick with it and try not to change it—the repetition over time is what gives it its power and meaning. After several years of saying The Jesus Prayer, I tried changing it once, to something similar, "Lord, Jesus Christ, Son of God, reveal Yourself to me, a seeker." It has the same flow, and points toward a meaningful goal— that of knowing the mind of Christ, but it didn't "take." The Jesus Prayer was too ingrained in me. Start with a phrase that is heartfelt and meaningful to you and stick with it. It may very well be the thing that helps you through your difficult time. It perhaps comes closest to what Paul meant when he said, "pray without ceasing" (1 Thessalonians 5:17).

PRAYER: Dear Lord, You are a God of mercy and love, and I seek to know You more fully. Let me consider this repetitive phrase as a way of knowing You, so that I might be drawn closer to You. In Jesus' name, amen.

---

286 The earliest written reference for this prayer is from *Discourse on Abba Philemon* from the *Philokalia*, "a collection of texts written between the 4th and 5th centuries by the spiritual masters" of the Eastern Orthodox church mystical Hesychast tradition.

156. RECIPROCITY WITH GOD

John 15:5. *I am the vine, you are the branches. Those who abide in me and I in them bear much fruit, because apart from me you can do nothing.*

There is a wonderful reciprocity uncovered in today's verse. God is the vine; we are the branches. Cut off from the vine, we die. But, likewise, if the vine lacks its branches, it can't fully display what it truly is. We are a precious part of God's creation, and we are the ones who help to display God's magnificence. Without us and our creativity, the world would not be nearly as exciting or interesting a place. God is the whole; we are the part. As Cynthia Bourgeault points out, "The part depends on the whole as its true source of identity and ongoing life. But the whole is equally dependent on the vibrant participation of the part in order to make its reality known. In this sense, they become "food" for each other, the one maintaining the other in a dynamic reciprocity."[287] Doesn't that give you an extra sense of "worth"? God depends on our vibrant participation with Him in order to be complete—we "complete" God! Certainly, we don't want to hide our talents in fear as the one servant did in the parable of the talents (Matthew 25:14-30). We want to go "full out" to use our talents for the glory of God. I hope that in your difficult time, you can rise above your difficulties to embrace this reciprocal relationship that we enjoy with God and live a fuller, complete life.

PRAYER: Dear Lord, I am encouraged by this concept of reciprocity with You. It gives me a new reason to thrive, knowing that I help complete Your creation. I so want to hear the words, "Well done, thou good and faithful servant" (Matthew 25:21 KJV) when I have completed my earthly assignment. No amount of difficulty that I face now can deter me from pleasing You. In Jesus' name, amen.

---

287 Cynthia Bourgeault, "Reciprocity with God," *Spirituality and Practice* webinar, Week 3, Session 2, October 31, 2012.

157. GIVING FROM OUR ABUNDANCE[288]

Matthew 25:40. *Truly I tell you, just as you did it to one of the least of these who are members of my family, you did it to me.*

We all want to be compassionate Christians. After all, that's what Jesus was all about, right? But sometimes it is hard to "muster up" compassion for others when we are so down-in-the-dumps with our difficult time. Here is an interesting thought from Cynthia Bourgeault, "Contrary to apparent logic, for Jesus, compassion is a *fruit* of [our] abundance, not a means to it."[289] In other words, we must first perceive our life to be one of abundance, out of which flows compassion, not be compassionate in order to somehow receive a reward of abundance. The trick is to see that you have an abundant life despite your difficulties. Everywhere you look, God's creation is flowing with abundance, if only we would open our eyes to see it! Take a walk in the woods or around a lake or pause to take a breath of fresh air. The plentiful supply of oxygen to feed our lungs is evidence enough of abundance, and there is so much more. Then, equipped with this insight, we can reach out to others with compassion. It is fundamental to the Christian walk. Remember Matthew 25:31-40, where the righteous ask Him, "When was it that we saw you hungry and gave you food" (they knew that they hadn't fed Him personally). He replied, "Truly I tell you, just as you did it to one of the least of these who are members of my family, you did it to me." Try to see abundance in your life, and, from it, let the compassion flow.

PRAYER: Dear Lord, I suspect that there have been times when I have reached out to others with "compassion" in order to reap some later reward for myself as if I were chalking up "brownie points" in the Kingdom of Heaven. This reflection has helped me reverse my thinking: compassion happens *after* I recognize the abundant life that I possess. Thank You for giving me so much and enabling me, as a result, to reach out to others. In Jesus' name, amen.

---

288 Cynthia Bourgeault, "Reciprocity with God," *Spirituality and Practice*, webinar, week 4 session 1, November 5, 2012; Portions paraphrased.
289 Bourgeault, webinar, week 4 session 1, November 5, 2012.

158. A BIG DISAPPOINTMENT

Romans 5:5. *And hope does not disappoint us, because God's love has been poured into our hearts through the Holy Spirit that has been given to us.*

I recently had a big disappointment that discouraged me. My application for a prestigious program that I very much wanted to participate in was turned down—a program that would have involved a two-year commitment on my part for which I was to devote a major portion of my efforts. As I sat down to read, God gave me this paragraph as a comfort:

Let this be a lesson to you in detachment from earthly things, for your better advance towards heaven. This has been allowed to happen to you to save you from falling into the mere enjoyment of spiritual things. God would have the Christian absolutely renounce all his desires and delights and attachments and to submit himself entirely to His divine will. He orders every event for the help and salvation of man; 'He willeth that all men should be saved.' Take courage then and believe that God 'will with the temptation provide also a way of escape' (1 Corinthians 10:13). Soon you will be rejoicing much more than you are now distressed.[290]

Perhaps I had thought that this program would do more for me than God could do through other means and was relying on its "prestige value" to "save me from the mere enjoyment of spiritual things." For whatever reason, God is choosing another path for me, which I must be alert and receptive to.

PRAYER: Dear Lord, Sometimes things don't go the way we want them to. Help us to see Your higher hand guiding us through life. In Jesus' name, amen.

---

290 Faith Annette Sand, *The Way of a Pilgrim and the Pilgrim Continues His Way*, trans. R. M. French (San Francisco: Harper, 1991), 22.

159. THE REDEMPTION OF ALL GOD'S CREATION[291]

Titus 2:14. [Christ] gave himself for us that he might redeem us from all iniquity and purify for himself a people of his own who are zealous for good deeds.

What if we have the question wrong? N.T. Wright says, "Rather than thinking that the main question is 'How can I get to heaven despite the sin because of which I deserve to be punished' (for which the answer is: 'because Jesus was punished in my place'), maybe the main question is, 'How can God's plan to rescue and renew the entire world go ahead despite the corruption and decay that have come about because of human rebellion?' (for which the answer is, 'because on the cross, Jesus defeated the powers of evil, which have enslaved rebel humans and so ensured continuing corruption.'")[292] Do you see the difference in focus? The first instance places the emphasis of salvation on us as *individuals*. The second places emphasis on the redemption of *all* of God's creation and our role in it. This change in perspective has profound implications for how we act here and now. We must be better stewards of this earth. We must seek social justice for those who have been wronged. We need to keep our difficult time in perspective by not being so concerned about ourselves but about our relationships with others and our respect for our mother earth, which we are to care for as agents of God. Yes, you are going through a difficult time, but when you think of the broader perspective of the suffering, decay, and redemption of all of creation, it may help you to cope.

PRAYER: Dear Lord, Help me to be a good steward of this earth. Let me not be so concerned about my own salvation, which has already been accomplished through You, but rather to be concerned with how I can be Your agent for the betterment of this world. In Jesus' name, amen.

---

291 N.T. Wright, *Surprised by Hope: Rethinking Heaven, the Resurrection, and the Mission of the Church* (New York: HarperOne, 2008), 199-200; Portions paraphrased.
292 Wright, 199.

160. THINGS CHANGE
BECAUSE GOD IS LOVE

1 John 4:8. *Whoever does not love does not know God, for God is love.*

Ilia Delio has caused me to rethink God's relationship to me and the world.[293] It is perhaps easiest to see God as the great Controller in the Sky, perfectly organized and planning the things of this Cosmos in infinite detail. However, Delio proposes a different construct: God does not "act" to cause things to change; rather, things change because God is love, and love is attractive. We have all experienced the freedom that true love brings—it does not attempt to control us but allows us the opportunity to be who we are, and, in that freedom, to please the other because of the very fact that we love them. I think that is what Delio is getting at here: God is loving us toward the optimal good. He is certainly in no hurry to do this, and He does not dictate the terms of how we will evolve. We are free to do so at our own pace and according to our own, God-given desires. "Our God is a God of self-emptying love, a God of humble love, who takes all the time in the world to create, a God who invites rather than forces the world to realize new possibilities of being."[294] I hope that this new way of seeing God resonates with you as it does for me. It puts a new "spin" on the difficulties we encounter: they are part and parcel of the way God loves us and helps us to grow despite our difficulties.

PRAYER: Dear Lord, It is comforting to me to reflect on the way that You love us into new ways of being rather than dictate our circumstances. Help me to relax and enjoy being in the presence of Your overwhelming love, so that I may grow in the direction You would have me grow. In Jesus' name, amen.

---

293 Ilia Delio, *The Humility of God: A Franciscan Perspective* (Cincinnati: St. Anthony Messenger Press, 2011), 838; Portions paraphrased.
294 Delio, 1403.

161. GOD LEARNS FROM US

Philippians 3:14. *I press on toward the goal for the prize of the heavenly call of God in Christ Jesus.*

Here's a pleasing thought—I'm not sure how theologically sound it is, but it resonates well with me—we surprise and delight God with *our* actions. God learns more about Himself in the way that we respond to Him, be it in obedience or evil. Since He has given us a free will, we are somewhat of a mystery to Him in the way we will react to life. God is vitally interested in the condition of our heart, and He is constantly seeking ways to be in relationship with us. Yes, I know that God is sovereign and unchanging and in ultimate control of our lives. But, the day-to-day living out of our dilemmas and joys is of vital interest to Him. He does not control what we do down to the last detail; we are not robots. Therefore, He must learn something of Himself by what we choose to do and how we are co-creators with Him in this mystery called life. I get some comfort in thinking this way. God and I are "partners." We learn from each other. He wants to know what is on my heart, and He takes pleasure in my obedience and feels pain when I stray. Take heart that God is vitally interested in your difficult circumstances and cares about you—and learns from you!

PRAYER: Dear Lord, I cherish the opportunity to be a "partner" and co-creator with You in life. Granted, I am Your child, but, just like a parent learns from its offspring, so too, do You learn from my decisions and creativity. May my obedience be pleasing to You, and my disobedience lead to confession and repentance so that I am a source of delight to You. In Jesus' name, amen.

162. SUMMARY

Galatians 2:19b-20. *I have been crucified with Christ; and it is no longer I who live, but it is Christ who lives in me. And the life I now live in the flesh I live by faith in the Son of God, who loved me and gave himself for me.*

I hope that you have enjoyed reading these reflections as much as I have enjoyed compiling them and that they have been a source of solace in your difficult time. It took me several years to research and prepare everything, a labor of love for those whom I knew would be uplifted by reading it. As you continue your journey, keep in mind that God is walking with you and is a constant source of comfort and hope. May your difficult time come to an end soon, and, in the meantime, may your prayer life and the love of fellow Christians sustain you.

PRAYER: Dear Lord, As my time with my reader draws to a close, I pray that You will comfort them and be a constant companion to help them in their time of difficulty. We are buoyed up by Your promise to love and be with us always. May it ever be so. In Jesus' name, amen.

BIBLIOGRAPHY

Bloom, Anthony. *Beginning to Pray*. New York: Paulist Press, 1970.

Buber, Martin. *I and Thou*. Translated by Ronald Gregor Smith. New York: Charles Scribner's Sons, 1958.

Bourgeault, Cynthia. "Reciprocity with God" webinar sponsored by *Spirituality and Practice*, Week 3, Session 2. October 31, 2012.

Brown, Brené. "The Power of Vulnerability." *TED Ideas Worth Spreading*. TEDxHouston, June 12, 2010.

Buechner, Frederick. *Listening To Your Life: Daily Meditations with Frederick Buechner*. Edited by George Conner. New York: Harper Collins, 1992.

Calvin, John. *Calvin: Institutes of the Christian Religion*. Edited by John T. McNeill. Louisville: Westminster John Knox Press, 1993.

Delio, Ilia, *The Humility of God: A Franciscan Perspective*. Cincinnati: St. Anthony Messenger Press, 2011.

Finley, James, *Merton's Palace of Nowhere*. Notre Dame: Ave Maria Press, 1978.

Guthrie, Shirley C., *Christian Doctrine*. Louisville: Westminster John Knox, 1994.

Harrison, Nick. *Promises to Keep: Daily Devotions for Men of Integrity*. San Francisco: HarperCollins, 1996.

Hemmingway, Ernest. *A Farewell to Arms*. New York: Scribner, 2012.

Jenkins, J. Jacob. *Buried Alive*. Baltimore: PublishAmerica, 2006.

Keating, Thomas. *The Daily Reader for Contemplative Reading: Excerpts from the Works of Father Thomas Keating*. New York: Continuum, 2006.

Lee, Peggy. "Is That All There Is?" Recorded 2001. Track 12 on *A Natural Woman*. Vinyl.

Marshall, Catherine. *The Helper*. Grand Rapids: Chosen Books, 2001. (reprint)

Martin, James, SJ. *The Jesuit Guide to (Almost) Everything: A Spirituality for Real Life*. New York: HarperCollins, 2010.

Milton, John. *Paradise Lost, Book I, Lines 221-270*. Poets.org. July 27, 2015. Accessed May 20, 2018. https://www.poets.org/poetsorg/poem/paradise-lost-book-i-lines-221-270.

Morley, Patrick. *Ten Secrets for the Man in the Mirror*. Grand Rapids: Zondervan, 2000.

Norwich, Julian of. *Revelations of Divine Love*. New York: Penguin Books, 1999.

Nouwen, Henry. *The Selfless Way of Christ: Downward Mobility and the Spiritual Life*. London: Darton, Longman and Todd, 2007.

Ortberg, John. *Faith and Doubt*. Grand Rapids: Zondervan, 2008.

Ortberg, John. *The Me I Want To Be: Becoming God's Best Version of You*. Grand Rapids: Zondervan, 2009.

Peterson, Eugene H. *A Long Obedience in the Same Direction*. Downers Grove: InterVarsity Press, 1980.

Peterson, Eugene H. *Practice Resurrection: A Conversation on Growing Up in Christ*. Grand Rapids: Wm. B. Eerdmans, 2010.

Peterson, Eugene H. *The Jesus Way: A Conversation on the Ways That Jesus Is the Way*. Grand Rapids: Wm. B. Eerdmans, 2007.

Pierce, Gregory F. Augustine. *Spirituality at Work: 10 Ways to Balance Your Life on the Job*. Chicago: Loyola Press, 2005.

Riso, Don Richard and Russ Hudson. *The Wisdom of the Enneagram: The Complete Guide to Psychological and Spiritual Growth for the Nine Personality Types*. New York: Bantam, 1999.

Rohr, Richard. *A Lever and a Place to Stand: The Contemplative Stance, The Active Prayer*. New York: Paulist Press, 2011.

Rohr, Richard. *Contemplation in Action*. New York: Crossroad, 2006.

Rohr, Richard. *Everything Belongs: The Gift of Contemplative Prayer*. New York: Crossroad, 2003.

Rohr, Richard. *Hope Against Darkness: The Transforming Vision of Saint Francis in an Age of Anxiety*. Cincinnati: St. Anthony Messenger Press, 2001.

Rohr, Richard. *Preparing for Christmas: Daily Meditations for Advent*. Cincinnati: St. Anthony Messenger Press, 2008.

Rohr, Richard. *Simplicity: The Art of Letting Go*. New York: Crossroad, 2004.

Rohr, Richard. *The Enneagram: A Christian Perspective*. New York: Crossroad, 2011.

Rohr, Richard. *The Naked Now: Learning To See As the Mystics See*. New York: Crossroad, 2009.

Rohr, Richard. *The Shape of God: Deepening the Mystery of the Trinity*. CD. Albuquerque: Center for Contemplation and Action, 2004.

Rohr, Richard. *Things Hidden: Scripture as Spirituality.* Cincinnati: St. Anthony Messenger Press, 2008.

Sand, Faith Annette. *The Way of a Pilgrim and The Pilgrim Loses His Way.* Translated by R. M. French. San Francisco: Harper, 1991.

Swindoll, Charles. *Strengthening Your Grip: How to Live Confidently in an Aimless World.* Nashville: Thomas Nelson, 2003.

Swindoll, Charles. *Persistence.* Radio. 1987.

Talbot, John Michael. *The Lessons of St. Francis: How to Bring Simplicity and Spirituality into Your Daily Life.* New York: Dutton, 1997.

Tutu, Desmond. *Made for Goodness: And Why This Makes All the Difference.* New York: HarperOne, 2010.

Walsh, Roger. *Essential Spirituality: The 7 Central Practices to Awaken Heart and Mind.* New York: John Wiley and Sons, 1999.

Willard, Dallas. *Hearing God: Developing a Conversational Relationship with God.* Downers Grove: InterVarsity Press, 1984.

Williamson, G.I. *The Westminster Shorter Catechism.* Phillipsburg: Presbyterian and Reformed Publishing Company, 2003.

Wright, N.T. *Lent for Everyone: Mark, Year B.* Louisville: Westminster John Knox Press, 2012.

Wright, N.T. *Lent for Everyone: Luke, Year C.* Louisville: Westminster John Knox Press, 2012.

Wright, N.T. *Surprised by Hope: Rethinking Heaven, the Resurrection, and the Mission of the Church.* New York: HarperOne, 2008.

For more information about

Ed Keelen
and
Helpful Reflections for Difficult Times
please visit:

www.facebook.com/HelpfulReflections

For more information about
AMBASSADOR INTERNATIONAL
please visit:

www.ambassador-international.com
@AmbassadorIntl
www.facebook.com/AmbassadorIntl

*If you enjoyed this book, please consider leaving us a review on
Amazon, Goodreads, or our website.*

Made in the USA
Middletown, DE
01 April 2020